How to Use Your Words

Übungsbuch

Lensing

Zusammengestellt und bearbeitet von Friedrich Pollmann

Mitwirkung und sprachliche Beratung: Timothy Sodmann

Illustrationen und Umschlaggestaltung: Christine Georg, Dortmund

> Zu diesem Übungsbuch ist erschienen:
> **How to Use Your Words**
> Lernwörterbuch in Sachgruppen
> ISBN 3–559–23300–3
> (siehe auch S. 88)

ISBN 3–559–**23254**–6

Alle Rechte vorbehalten

© 1987 Verlag Lambert Lensing GmbH, Dortmund

Herstellung: Ernst Knoth GmbH, Melle
Printed in Germany

Das Werk und seine Teile sind urheberrechtlich geschützt. Jede Verwertung in anderen als den gesetzlich zugelassenen Fällen bedarf der vorherigen schriftlichen Einwilligung des Verlags.

Druck A $^{5\ 4\ 3\ 2}$ / Jahr 1996 95 94 93 92

Die letzte Zahl bezeichnet das Jahr des Druckes. Alle Drucke der Serie A sind gegenüber der Auflage 1/87 unverändert und daher im Unterricht parallel verwendbar.

Hinweise für den Lehrer

Das Übungsbuch im Verbund

Das vorliegende Übungsbuch ist ein Arbeitsmittel zur Wortschatzarbeit in der Schule. Es ergänzt das Lernwörterbuch *How to Use Your Words* und das gleichnamige CALL-Programm für den Mikrocomputer Commodore C 64 bzw. C 128. Während Lernwörterbuch und Vokabellernprogramm vor allem den ständig fortgeführten Neuerwerb des Wortschatzes unterstützen, hat das Übungsbuch die Festigung und – besonders in höheren Klassen bzw. Kursen – die Reaktivierung des bereits Gelernten zum Ziel.

Das Übungsbuch im Gebrauch

Das Übungsbuch wendet sich an Schüler und Schülerinnen ab etwa Klasse 9; es kann bis in die Oberstufe hinein benutzt werden. Das breite Angebot an Sachbereichen und Übungen, zu überschaubaren Übungseinheiten zusammengefaßt, berücksichtigt sowohl Erfahrungsbereiche als auch sprachliche Kenntnisse und Fertigkeiten unterschiedlicher Lerngruppen. Neben dem Üben der Bildung, Schreibung und Bedeutung von Einzelwörtern wird entsprechend der Zielsetzung des Lernwörterbuchs auch im Übungsbuch besonderer Wert auf die Festigung des Wortgebrauchs gelegt. Zahlreiche Rätsel, Geschichten und Illustrationen unterstützen das Lernen auf unterhaltsame Weise.
Die systematisch von einer Übungseinheit zur nächsten fortschreitende Wiederholung und Festigung des Wortschatzes ohne inhaltlichen Bezug zum Unterricht wird in der Schule eher die Ausnahme sein. Die Zuordnung der Übungseinheiten zu überschaubaren Sachbereichen erleichtert die Anbindung an konkrete Unterrichtsinhalte. Wie die Übungen im einzelnen bearbeitet werden, ob mündlich oder schriftlich, von der ganzen Lerngruppe gemeinsam im Gespräch darüber, in Gruppenarbeit oder einzeln, bleibt in vielen Fällen der Entscheidung des Unterrichtenden überlassen. Bei einigen Übungen ist es am besten, gleich in das Übungsbuch hineinzuschreiben, z.B. um die in den *letter grids* gefundenen Wörter zu markieren oder um fehlende Präpositionen einzusetzen. In jedem Fall ist es sinnvoll, ein eigenes Heft zur Wortschatzarbeit führen zu lassen.
Nicht alle der ca. 7000 Wörter des Sachwörterbuchs, sondern nur die wichtigeren konnten im Übungsbuch berücksichtigt werden. Vollständigkeit hätte bei vielen Sachbereichen zu überlangen Übungseinheiten geführt. Lücken können auch durch selbst erstellte Übungen nach dem Vorbild des Übungsbuchs gefüllt werden. Diese könnten auch von den Schülern als Hausaufgabe entworfen und in der folgenden Stunde untereinander getauscht und bearbeitet werden, z.B. mit der Arbeitsanweisung: "Here are ten words not included in the exercises we've done today. For your homework would you design an exercise in which they fit best?"

Zu den Lösungen

Auf durchgehende Lösungsangaben wurde verzichtet. Ein genaueres Studium des in *How to Use Your Words* zusammengetragenen Wortmaterials führt in der Regel zur richtigen Lösung. Grundsätzlich gilt, daß immer nur die Lösungen gemeint sind, die in die jeweils am Anfang einer Übungseinheit genannten Sachbereiche passen. Bei Zuordnungsübungen, wie z.B. bei denen mit der Arbeitsanweisung *Match the words*, sollten die einzelnen *items* nicht isoliert betrachtet werden. Zwar gibt es oft mehr als eine Möglichkeit, Wörter miteinander zu verknüpfen. Damit der Schüler aber selbständig zu einer insgesamt richtigen Lösung finden kann, sind diese Übungen so angelegt, daß alle Wörter verwendet werden müssen, aber nur einmal verwendet werden dürfen. Deshalb wird in der Arbeitsanweisung immer vermerkt: *Use each item only once*. Ist eine Wortverbindung nicht zulässig, wird der Schüler spätestens bei den beiden zuletzt verbleibenden *items* merken, daß er irgendwo einen Fehler gemacht hat, es sei denn, er identifiziert fälschlicherweise auch diese als „richtig". Die *letter grids* sind mit Hilfe eines Computerprogramms erstellt worden. So kann es im Einzelfall vorkommen, daß zusätzlich zu den jeweils zehn versteckten Wörtern zufällig noch ein weiteres Wort des betreffenden Sachbereichs gefunden werden kann. Bei der Bearbeitung der Aufgaben und der Besprechung der Lösungen ergeben sich vielfältige Möglichkeiten zur Einübung von Sprechabsichten. Diese sollte man immer nutzen, um die Wortschatzstunden lebendig zu gestalten.

Friedrich Pollmann, Coesfeld
Timothy Sodmann, Billerbeck

Inhaltsangabe

Ourselves (Sachgruppen 1–44) 7

    Man, person 7
    Person 8
    Body 9
    Senses (a) 12
    Senses (b) 13
    Positions, movements of the body (a) 14
    Positions, movements of the body (b) 15
    Eating and drinking (a) 16
    Eating and drinking (b) 17
    Health, illness 18
    Clothing 19
    Mental life (a) 20
    Mental life (b) 21
    Mental life (c) 23

Ourselves and the others (Sachgruppen 45–104) 25

    Communication (a) 25
    Communication (b) 26
    Language 28
    Literature 30
    The mass media 31
    Our relations with others 33
    Our family 34
    Church 36
    Our school 37
    Our country (a) 39
    Our country (b) 41
    Our country (c) 41
    Society 43

Our working life (Sachgruppen 105–119) 44
    Work (a) 44
    Work (b) 45
    Production 46
    Trade 48
    Money 49

Our leisure time (Sachgruppen 120–132) 51
    Holidays 51
    Sports and games 52
    Art and entertainment 55

The world around us (Sachgruppen 133–186) 57
    Our home (a) 57
    Our home (b) 58
    Our town, our village 60
    Transport 62
    Animals around us 64
    Plants around us 66
    Earth (a) 68
    Earth (b) 70
    Universe 71
    Matter 73
    Existence (a) 75
    Existence (b) 76
    Existence (c) 77

The order in our world (Sachgruppen 187–201) 78
    Number 78
    Time (a) 81
    Time (b) 82
    Space (a) 83
    Space (b) 85

ourselves

man, person

1 man · 2 sex · 3 name · 4 age

1. *What are the words? Fill in the missing letters to find them.*

m __ n; w __ m __ n; b __ y; g __ rl; s __ r; l __ dy; n __ m __ ; b __ rthd __ y; y __ __ ng; __ ld; ch __ ld

2. *Connect each word with its definition.*

age, childhood, introduce, mankind, nobody, old age, race, sign, surname, youth

a) group of people of the same colour; b) another word for "no one"; c) all human beings; d) another word for "family name"; e) the time when you were a child; f) how old you are; g) the time when you are old; h) to make known to each other; i) to write your name at the end of a letter; j) the time of your life when you are young

3. *Choose the word that best fits the context.*

a) In America there were many different ... (races / tribes) of Indians. b) Europeans belong to a different ... (people / race) than Chinese. c) There were a lot of ... (persons / people) at the football match. d) We all like him because he is a good ... (fellow / man).

4. Older, elder, *or* eldest? *Fill in the right word.*

a) Sheila: "Tom is my younger brother." Tom: "Sheila is my _____ sister." b) Mother: "Sheila is the _____ of the two." c) Father: "Yes, she's three years _____ than Tom." d) Aunt Lucy: "We were five children, I was the _____. I was only one year _____ than your Uncle Tim."

5. *Fill in the missing prepositions:* at, by, in, like, on, to

a) behave _____ a gentleman; b) know a person _____ name; c) put your signature _____ a letter; d) _____ my 16th birthday; e) _____ the age of 18; f) _____ my youth

6. *How would you begin a letter to ... ?*

a) Tim Harris. Tim is a good friend of yours. b) Mr Wilkinson. He manages a language school in Brighton. You want to know details about the courses that his school is offering this year. c) The Halifax Building Society. You've read their ad in THE OBSERVER and would like further information.

person

5 life · 6 death

1. *What are the things?*

2. *Fill in the missing words.*

a) More than 3,000 people lost their ... when in 1953 the dams broke in Holland. b) Uncle George ... all his brothers and sisters and is 83 now. c) Tim ... a lot of money from his aunt when she died. d) A man and two children were ... in a car accident last night. e) All over the world thousands of people ... of hunger each year, so help is necessary. f) The cat was playing with a ... mouse and then killed it. g) In her will the old lady ... everything to her dog. h) He was ... in the village churchyard. i) He has been ... since 1982.

3. *Fill in the missing prepositions:* for, in, of, of, of, on, to

a) the American way _____ life; b) live _____ $800 a month; c) die _____ hunger; d) be killed _____ an accident; e) mourn _____ a good friend; f) be heir _____ the throne; g) be tired _____ life

4. *Read the story and the report and make a list of the missing words.*

Life ...

Robinson Crusoe led an exciting ... . Once he made a voyage to South America. When his ship was a few miles off the Orinoko River, a violent storm rose and drove him off course onto a sandbank. Robinson and the crew got into a boat, but the boat capsized in the huge waves and all but Robinson lost their ... . Robinson was tossed on a rock. More ... than ... he tried to get onto his feet. Before the next wave could get at him, he was able to jump up and began to run for his ... . The next morning he looked for the others, but in vain. He was the only ... . His ... was a wonder. Of course, he was happy that he was still ... , but where was he and would a ship ever find him? Soon he found out that he was shipwrecked on an uninhabited island and that he was the only ... being there excepting a few goats and birds. By and then it dawned on him that he was very likely to ... the rest of his ... on the island and he felt so miserable that he even thought of ... his own life.

... and death

The snowmobile – a deadly weapon?
Today there are 2,000,000 snowmobiles in North America, but there is a tragic side to the snowmobile's success. In 1969, for example, the first year snowmobile accidents were surveyed, 93 ... were recorded. In 1970, as many as 127 Canadians ... in snowmobile accidents, among them four people who were ... when their snowmobiles collided with parked cars. Two more ... in collisions while driving on the wrong side of the road. Typical was the case of a snowmobiler driving onto freshly frozen ice where a ferry boat had recently tried to reach an island. He plunged to his .... His ... has never been found. Six snowmobilers were stranded 45 miles from home when their two vehicles broke down. Five walked back, one stayed behind. He froze to ....

body

7 figure · 8 head, hair · 9 face, looks · 10 parts of the face · 11 trunk · 12 limbs · 13 organs and their functions

1. *Which sentence fits which picture?*

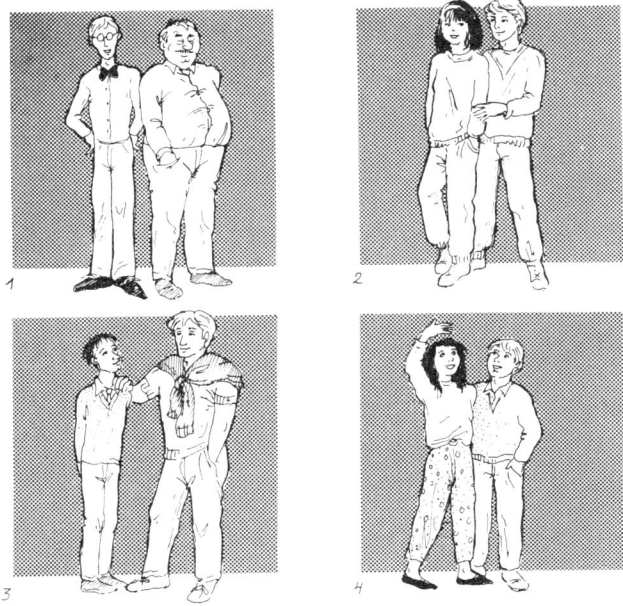

a) Jean and Thomas are tall.
b) John is thin. Tom is fat.
c) Mary and Henry are short.
d) Tim is small. Ronald is big.

2. *Hidden words: Find the ten words for parts of the face. Look for them in all directions of the grid.*

R	G	S	A	H	X	I	Y	X	M	E	M
F	O	R	E	H	E	A	D	O	Z	A	S
P	K	Y	F	H	X	J	U	C	F	R	A
S	S	I	T	J	A	T	F	Y	X	G	C
T	C	A	M	W	H	N	E	S	O	N	H
Y	X	T	I	X	L	B	S	F	D	Q	E
G	E	G	U	I	X	G	T	T	V	K	E
M	O	Y	E	Y	E	S	F	J	F	X	K
K	P	B	E	W	U	G	U	M	P	Q	J
H	O	S	Z	L	O	M	P	W	F	P	U
R	M	H	T	U	I	R	J	J	G	F	Q
K	O	C	H	I	N	D	B	U	J	N	B

3. *Name the parts of the body.*

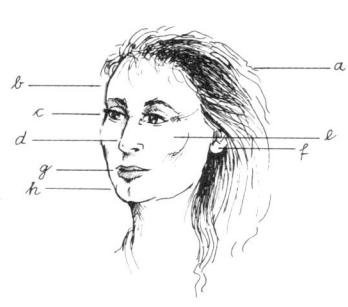

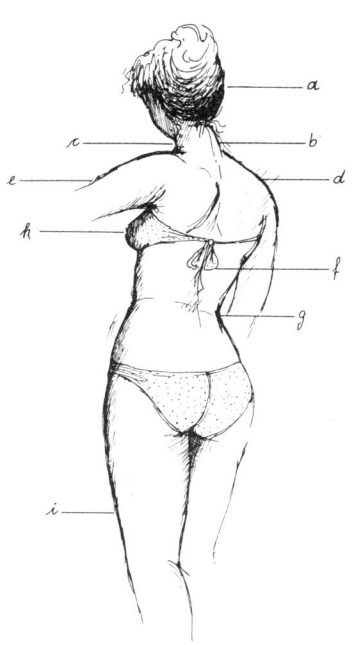

4. *Name the parts of the hand.*   **5.** *Name the parts of the foot.*

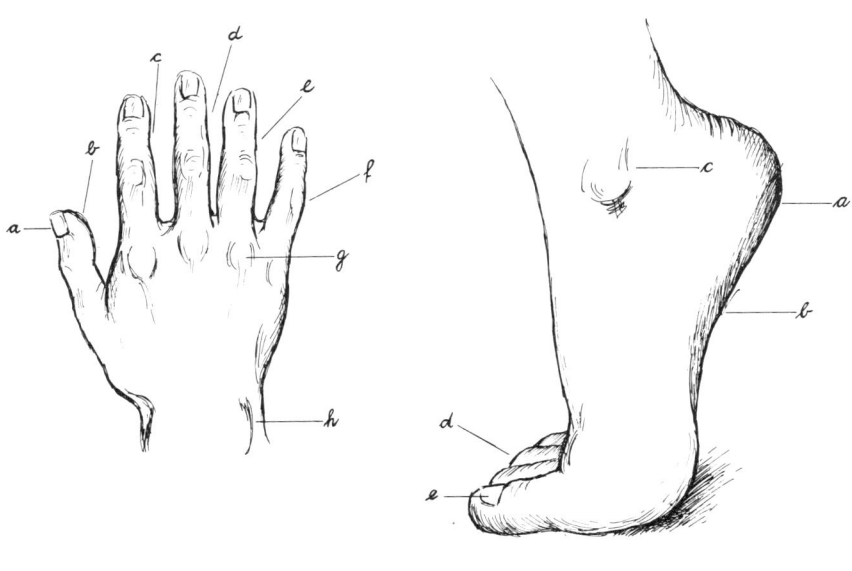

6. *Find the right words.*

a) The old man fell over the empty whisky bottle and broke several .... b) The knee is a ... in the leg, the elbow is a ... in the arm. c) The ... is the organ which pumps blood round the body. d) We take air into the ... through the nose and mouth.

7. *Which words often go together? Use each item only once.*

What people look like. They have (a/an) ...

        a oval / round   1 ... nose
        b long / short   2 ... face
        c thin / thick   3 ... feet
        d fair / brown   4 ... back
        e ruddy / chubby   5 ... skin
        f large / big   6 ... legs
        g broad / narrow   7 ... hair
        h straight / bent   8 ... shoulders
        i long / flat   9 ... lips
        j greasy / dry   10 ... cheeks

8. *Make sentences to show that you understand the meaning of the following words.*

a) features; b) complexion; c) freckle; d) wrinkle; e) neck; f) throat

senses (a)

14 sight

1. *Hidden words: Find the ten words for colours that are hidden in the letter grid. Look for them in all directions.*

Q	C	X	I	X	I	K	M	S	Y	H	T
O	R	A	N	G	E	A	N	V	D	Q	P
P	M	L	V	Y	F	H	Q	O	I	U	I
I	E	J	X	O	E	Q	Z	J	Y	F	U
N	T	G	V	C	P	L	O	M	T	B	E
K	I	Q	S	R	J	S	L	Y	E	R	G
Y	H	R	N	I	G	S	N	O	J	O	I
N	W	Q	R	B	R	E	D	E	W	W	Z
X	Q	O	L	N	B	E	M	G	E	N	T
O	Y	A	T	Z	U	K	Q	W	X	R	R
V	C	G	Z	L	L	P	T	P	H	W	G
K	H	X	B	C	N	W	T	E	M	R	H

2. *What are the words? Put in the missing letters to find them.*

s __ g __ t; __ li __ __ ; wa __ __ h; __ __ arc __ ; __ pp __ ar; c __ l __ __ r; __ l __ e; sh __ __ __ w; fl __ s __ ; __ rig __ __

3. *Complete the sentences with their parts from the list below.*

a) I can't read ... b) You must ... c) The men in the boat ... d) I've been looking for my keys ... e) I couldn't find him because he had ... f) The old man's ... g) It's very hot today; let's sit ... h) Sailors wear ... i) The sea looked beautiful ... j) There was a flash of lightning ...

1 hidden behind a tree. 2 in the moonlight. 3 which lit up the whole neighbourhood. 4 look before you cross the road. 5 hair was white. 6 dark blue clothes. 7 without my glasses. 8 in the shade under the tree. 9 sighted land. 10 and now I've found them.

4. *Which words often go together? Use each item only once.*

a	wear	1	... for your ticket
b	watch	2	... a glimpse of
c	observe	3	... TV
d	examine	4	... a shadow
e	find	5	... glasses
f	catch	6	... land
g	throw	7	... the stars
h	light	8	... a patient
i	sight	9	... a cigarette
j	search	10	... what you've lost

5. *Fill in the missing prepositions:* at, by, from, in (4x), into, off, on, on

a) blind _____ one eye; b) put _____ your glasses; c) look _____ a picture; d) come _____ sight; e) it is _____ view; f) hide it _____ Jean; g) _____ dark colours; h) switch _____ the lights; i) _____ the sunshine; j) _____ the dark; k) dazzled _____ the lights of a car

6. *What is your favourite colour? What colour do you not like at all?*

senses (b)
15 hearing · 16 smell · 17 taste · 18 touch

1. *What are the words? The letters of the following words have been arranged alphabetically. Put them in the right order again.*
aer; eilnst; dlou; inosy; ellms; eestw; beirtt; eefl; aestt; iknst

2. *Word scrabble: Find the missing words and fill the squares with them.*

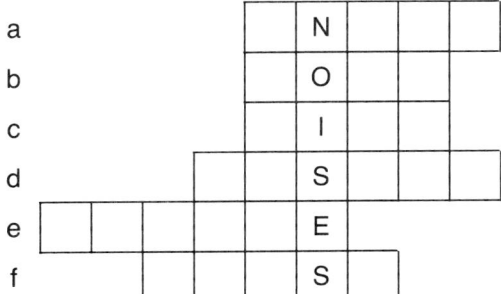

Here is some help:
a I heard a ... at the door.
b Lions and tigers ... when they are angry.
c When you get to the house, ... the doorbell.
d Dead leaves ... when the wind blows.
e I heard the ... of the empty milk bottles.
f Did you hear the ...
  when the car drove
  into the lamppost?

3. *Which words often go together? Use each item only once.*

a	sweet	1	... sea water
b	acid	2	... honey
c	sour	3	... curry
d	bitter	4	... milk
e	salty	5	... vinegar
f	hot	6	... coffee

4. *Which of these words fits the situation best:* touch, feel, *or* handle? *Change their form if necessary.*

a) The doctor ... my arm to find out if it was broken. b) The river was so deep that I could not ... the bottom. c) When the lights went out, we had to ... along the wall to find the door. d) Wash your hands before you ... the new book. e) Please do not ... the paintings. f) Suddenly I ... a sharp pain in my back. g) Glass! ... with care!

positions, movements of the body (a)

19 positions, changing one's position · 20 moving from place to place

1. *Which sentence fits which picture?*

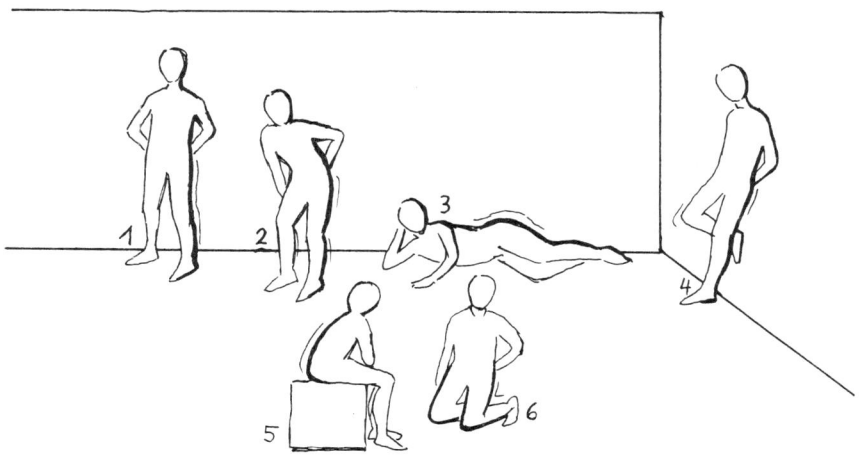

a) He is leaning against a wall. b) He is sitting. c) He is kneeling. d) He is bending forward. e) He is lying. f) He is standing.

2. *What are the words? Re-order the letters to find them.*

meco; og; lawk; pets; urn; cbmli; crpee; pho; pils; lafl

3. *Choose the word that best fits the context.*

a) There is no bus so we ... (go / walk) to school. b) I slipped on the ice and ... (fell over / dropped). c) A thief ... (crawled / crept) into the house at night. d) She ... (hopped / jumped) to her feet and ran out of the room. e) Baby is learning to walk and often ... (limps / trips). f) The old man ... (slipped / slid) on the icy road. g) The football player hurt his foot and ... (staggered / limped) off the field.

4. *What may cause or lead you to ...*

a) lean out of the window? b) rise from your seat? c) jump out of bed? d) turn your head towards another person? e) lie still? f) tiptoe to the baby's bed? g) trip up the stairs? h) run after somebody? i) pace the platform up and down? j) hop on one leg?

5. *Fill in the missing prepositions:* for, from, in, on (4x), onto, over, to, up, with

a) arrive _____ London; b) get _____ London by 3 o'clock; c) go _____ foot; d) go _____ a walk; e) keep step _____ somebody; f) hurry _____ the stairs; g) trip _____ the carpet; h) walk _____ tiptoe; i) hop _____ one leg; j) slip _____ an icy road; k) fall _____ a tree; l) climb _____ a roof

positions, movements of the body (b)
21 holding on to or letting go · 22 touching and moving

1. *Hidden words: Put a ring round the ten verbs hidden in the grid. Look for them in all directions.*

F	A	M	H	O	L	D	I	T	Y	X	U
C	W	W	P	W	J	T	G	R	A	S	P
N	Z	Q	Z	Y	R	R	A	C	W	D	T
Q	V	G	Y	W	E	N	B	K	U	V	F
S	I	J	H	E	T	X	Y	C	E	Z	I
V	D	E	S	M	K	G	H	H	Q	G	L
N	G	C	F	V	K	X	S	N	A	Z	E
B	T	U	L	U	M	U	H	L	B	S	T
G	I	T	I	A	P	V	K	C	E	U	N
J	K	L	N	X	S	R	Y	I	U	U	V
H	B	O	K	E	D	P	Z	A	O	O	T
B	Y	I	H	I	F	E	X	R	L	H	T

2. *Change the order of the letters to find the words.*

eszie; pta; rrcya; edbn; hkase; spamt; tres; tifl; rsocs; lfdo

3. *Choose the word that best fits the context.*

a) She ... (tapped / knocked) him on the shoulder and he turned round. b) He ... (thrust / threw) the ball to me. c) She ... (stamped / kicked) upstairs in anger. d) I entered the lift and ... (pressed / pushed) the button for the 12th floor. e) The dog woke up and ... (stretched / spread) itself. f) Mary ... (wiped / rubbed) the table for Mother. g) ... (Pick up / Raise) your hand when you want to speak.

4. *Find at least one verb which can be used with each of the following.*

a) ... your head / your eyes / your hand; b) ... a cushion / a bottle of medicine; c) ... your nose / your shoes; d) ... your knees / your arms / a piece of wire; e) ... your eyes / your mouth / the door; f) ... a knife / a gun / a card from a pack

5. *What may cause you to ...*

a) rest your head on your hands? b) lay the newspaper aside? c) stamp your feet? d) push yourself to the front? e) rub your eyes? f) stretch out your legs? g) grope your way to a seat in a cinema? h) let go your grip on a rope? i) drop a pan? j) lose hold of your umbrella?

eating and drinking (a)

23 eat, drink, digest · 25 meals

1. *Draw pictures to show how they are different.*

a) fork and knife; b) plate and saucer; c) cup and bowl; d) jug and glass; e) teaspoon and table-spoon

2. *What do you ... ?*

boil; bake; roast; fry; cook; cut; slice; chop; peel; stew

3. *Fill in the right words from this list:* bite, chew, choke, drink, eat, feed, lick, swallow. *Change their forms if necessary.*

a) He tried to ... , but his throat was too dry. b) If you ... a lot of cake you will get fat. c) Don't ... off more than you can ... . d) Always ... your food well before swallowing it. e) I've ... all the wine. f) She ... the baby with a spoon. g) His death was sudden: he ... on a fish bone. h) The child ... the ice cream cone.

4. *Meals through the day. Which meals can you have when and what are they called? Put together your own appropriate menu for each meal.*

Time of day: morning, mid-morning, noon, afternoon, evening / night, any time

Name of meal: tea, dinner / supper, snack, lunch, breakfast, brunch

Things to eat and drink (if anything is missing, just add it to your list): cornflakes, soup, porridge, bacon and eggs, toast, cake, chips, potatoes, vegetables, fish, sweets, scrambled eggs, tea, coffee, sausages, dessert, steak, sandwich, ice cream, roll, butter, jam, marmalade, chop, salad, roast beef, wine, ale

eating and drinking (b)

24 food and drink

1. *What are the words? Put in the missing letters to find them.*

__ea;   c__ea__;   __tea__;   __eal;   __eat;   b__ea__;   ____f__ee;

b_____r; h__ne__;   __eef; c__ee__e

2. *Odd man out: Which word does not belong to the others?*

a bread – loaf – roll – cake
b ale – wine – milk – beer
c sausage – veal – beef – pork
d jam – cheese – marmalade – honey
e coffee – egg – milk – sugar

3. *Let's play charades: Find ten words for things you can eat or drink by putting the pieces together again.*

ade – age – choco – cof – ey – fee – ga – hon – lade – late – lem – ma – mar – mar – mus – on – pas – por – ridge – rine – saus – tard – try

4. *Letter row: Put a line under the ten hidden words for things you can eat or drink. They are written in this direction:* →

g d h r t j a e a m j a m o i u c s h o p c h o p e i t e a f s
b i e r a l l e b r e d a l e s w a s i c e a e m i n e r t s t
e v i n e s e l t p i e w a t e c a c e h a m p s h i r e e a x
e a r n i b e k i e w i n e g r h s g d f e r s a u s a g e r s
i s w e a t s a u e r p o r k s m r s q u a s h e s t d f e f p

5. *Here are some English proverbs with words for things to eat or drink. Match them with the following explanations.*

1 You cannot sell the cow and drink the milk.
2 Half a loaf is better than no bread.
3 One man's meat is another man's poison.
4 Jam tomorrow and jam yesterday – but no jam today.
5 Better an egg today than a hen tomorrow.
6 Do not put new wine in old bottles.

a) One person may like what another may hate. b) You must have one thing or the other, not both. c) We should not try to bring together things which are out of keeping with each other. d) If there is one day of the week that we enjoy more than the other six, today never seems to be that day. e) It is better to accept something small than to reject it and hope to get more later on. f) We should be thankful for what we receive, even though it is not as much as we had hoped for.

health, illness

27 health, illness · 28 accident · 29 at the doctor's · 30 at the dentist's

1. *Hidden words: Put a ring round the ten hidden words used when talking about a person's health or illness. They are written in all directions.*

Q	T	O	F	K	O	W	S	P	Q	A	L
T	O	O	T	H	A	C	H	E	Z	V	O
Q	R	M	I	H	D	N	U	U	G	K	D
C	D	V	D	L	E	S	Q	R	T	E	N
M	V	E	O	O	I	A	M	J	N	C	R
E	C	C	E	S	P	B	D	T	Y	M	L
D	F	M	T	L	Y	H	I	A	W	N	I
I	R	P	H	H	B	S	G	X	C	L	R
C	G	A	G	T	T	W	Y	X	L	H	Q
I	M	I	U	O	Y	Q	T	V	I	P	E
N	Z	N	O	L	I	E	R	U	J	N	I
E	G	H	C	X	X	H	Q	P	X	N	E

2. *Here are some English proverbs. Can you explain what they mean? How would you translate them into your own language? If possible, use a proverb. But before ... fill in the missing words.*

a) ... is better than wealth. b) The tongue ever turns to the ... tooth. c) No gain without .... d) A ... child dreads the fire. e) Never tell your enemy that your foot .... f) Time is the great .... g) Early to bed and early to rise makes a man ... , wealthy, and wise.

3. *What are the words? Put in* ee, ea, *or* ai *to find them.*

w_____k; sn_____ze; h_____lth; p_____n; bl_____d; dis_____se; spr_____n; tr_____t

4. *Match the verbs on the left with the nouns on the right. Use each item only once.*

    a catch   1 ... a wound
    b see   2 ... a cold
    c treat   3 ... a plaster
    d have   4 ... a doctor
    e dress   5 ... an injection
    f give   6 ... an X-ray
    g make   7 ... a tooth
    h put on   8 ... an accident
    i pull   9 ... a patient

clothing

31 clothes · 32 clothing requisites and jewellery · 33 materials, fashion, making clothes · 34 wearing clothes · 35 keeping clothes in order

1. *Draw pictures to show how they are different.*

a) cap and hat; b) shirt and pullover; c) braces and belt; d) trousers and shorts; e) shoe and glove; f) wallet and purse; g) handbag and briefcase; h) bracelet and necklace; i) brooch and ring; j) hanky and scarf; k) zip and button

2. *Name the things shown in the pictures.*

3. *Which of the following things are usually worn only by men, only by women, or by men and women?* shirt; blouse, braces; bra; dress; jacket; suit; slip; dinner jacket; evening gown; raincoat

4. *Which verb goes with which noun ? Use each item only once.*

    a darn   1 ... a suit
    b do   2 ... a pullover
    c drop   3 ... a button
    d knit   4 ... a tie
    e knot   5 ... a sock
    f mend   6 ... the washing
    g polish   7 ... a hole
    h press   8 ... a shoe
    i put on   9 ... a needle
    j sew on   10 ... a ring
    k tailor   11 ... a shirt
    l thread   12 ... a stitch

mental life (a)

36 mind · 37 thinking · 38 understanding, knowledge

1. *Let's play charades: Find ten words by putting the pieces together again.*

ar – at – ble – cer – con – cov – dis – er – er – ex – fa – gence – i – ig – in – li – mil – no – plore – rant – rea – sen – si – sid – son – tain – tel – ten – tion

2. *What are the words? Fill in the blanks with the missing letters to find them.*

A person may be described as intelligent or ...

__ __ e __ er, __ m __ rt, br ____ ht, g __ ft __ __ .

A person may be described as unintelligent or ...

__ u __ l, fo ____ is __ , __ tu ____ d, or just s __ ll __ .

3. *Which words usually go together? Use each item only once.*

    a explore   1 ... the news
    b discover   2 ... French
    c find   3 ... a country
    d get   4 ... a secret
    e pay   5 ... an answer
    f know   6 ... what has happened
    g talk   7 ... the joke
    h show   8 ... sense
    i make   9 ... attention
    j see   10 ... presence of mind

4. *Put in the missing prepositions.*

a) listen _____ reason; b) toy _____ an idea; c) be ignorant _____ Latin; d) be _____ doubt about what to do; e) come _____ an understanding; f) make sure _____ the time; g) be clever _____ repairing cars; h) be _____ low spirits; i) bore your listeners _____ death; j) have a great gift _____ music

5. *Which adjectives can you derive from the following words?*

attention; mind; bore; gift; intelligence; sense; reason; thought; doubt; understand; know; comprehend

mental life (b)

39 traits, feelings, forms of behaviour

1. *Hidden words: Put a ring round the ten hidden adjectives that can be used to describe a person's behaviour. They are written in all directions.*

H	G	Y	O	L	S	O	C	H	Y	T	F
F	A	I	T	H	F	U	L	H	B	K	G
S	Z	R	E	S	C	O	L	D	S	I	B
L	Y	D	J	N	E	Q	S	X	W	R	A
Q	U	T	N	C	P	L	W	R	A	V	I
R	T	V	S	X	J	Y	F	V	N	Q	H
H	I	D	Q	A	Q	O	E	I	R	K	N
O	U	J	R	V	N	X	P	M	S	F	G
N	X	U	R	J	M	N	M	O	P	H	L
E	R	S	I	Z	G	M	E	W	T	V	P
S	Q	T	A	I	C	T	L	E	U	R	C
T	Q	O	F	M	Y	X	U	I	T	Q	Z

21

2. *What does he look like? He looks ....*

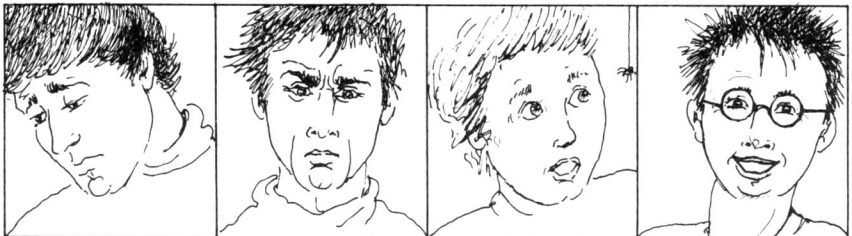

3. *What are the words? Find the missing letters and fill the squares with them.*

a ... F ...
b ... E ...
c ... E ...
d ... L ...
e ... I ...
f ... N ...
g ... G ...

Here is some help:
a She is always ... and smiling.
b I like him – he is a very ... person.
c Thank you: you were very ....
d I'm ... that you are better.
e That's not ....
f Why are you so ... ?
g Don't be ... !

4. *Which words usually go together? Use each item only once.*

a true
b fair
c hopeless
d violent
e good
f friendly
g strict
h horrible
i careless
j misleading

1 a ... quarrel
2 on ... terms
3 a ... sight
4 in ... confidence
5 a ... case
6 a ... friend
7 a ... driver
8 a ... play
9 a ... statement
10 ... manners

5. *Choose the word that best fits the context.*

a) It is bad ... (manners / conduct) to stare at people. b) The film was very ... (pleasing / amusing) and we laughed a lot. c) Jean wished us a ... (Happy / Merry) New Year. d) Many stories have a ... (glad / happy) ending. e) I'm sorry to ... (disappoint / complain of) you, but I can't come. f) How do you ... (love / like) it ? g) We are on ... (friendly / nice) terms with him. h) He has a pleasant manner and makes ... (friendships / friends) easily. i) It is not ... (respectable / respectful) to be drunk in the street. j) He holds ... (modest / moderate) political opinions. k) It is not ... (just / fair) to kick another player in football.

6. *"A friend in need is a friend indeed." Find the missing words.*

Your real friend ...

a) never tells a secret if you have taken him into your ... . b) always ... you in an argument. c) can be ... on to do what he has promised. d) can be ... . e) can always be ... on for help. f) You can always ... upon his help.

A false friend is one ...

a) who hardly ever ... with you in an argument. b) who you can put no ... in. c) who is scarcely ... to his words. d) who does not remain ... to you.

7. *Qualities: Which is the most important quality*
  a) a good friend of yours,
  b) your teachers,
  c) your parents,
  d) a politician
  should have in your opinion?

a) be trustworthy; b) be strong-willed; c) be patient; d) be intelligent; e) be nice; f) be helpful; g) be honest; h) be modest; i) be imaginative; j) be determined; k) be cheerful; l) be well-behaved; m) be tactful

8. *Qualities: Which of the following qualities would you dislike most in a person?*

a) be ignorant; b) be stupid; c) be indifferent; d) be arrogant; e) be conceited; f) be impudent; g) be selfish; h) be weak-willed; i) be cruel

mental life (c)

40 imagination · 41 memory · 42 will · 43 plans · 44 opinion

1. *Put in the missing letters to complete the words.*

__ m __ g __ n __ ; r __ m __ mb __ r; w __ nt; w __ sh; pl __ n; __ d __ __ ; __ rd __ r; c __ mm __ nd; m __ m __ ry; r __ m __ nd; s __ pp __ s __

2. *Syllable scrabble: Put the pieces together again to find the words defined below.*

be – con – con – de – de – di – ent – er – for – fuse – get – ion – mand – mem – nize – o – o – o – og – pin – re – rec – ry – sid – sire – vince

a to wish or want very much
b the ability to remember things or persons
c not to remember, not to bring with you
d to ask very strongly for something
e to think over carefully
f willing to obey
g be not willing to do
h that which a person thinks about something
i to cause someone to believe
j to know somebody or something again

3. *Complete the sentences with the following words:* ask, eager, forget, idea, imagine, intend, remember, tell, think, want. *Change their form when necessary.*

a) ... the children to be quiet. b) That's a difficult question; I've no ... of the answer. c) I ... my umbrella, and got very wet when it rained. d) I ... to go to Spain next month. e) The customs officer ... for my passport. f) Can you ... how he feels? g) The boys are ... to play football this afternoon. h) I ... you to come and help me. i) He gave me his phone number, but I can't ... it. j) "Will it rain?" – "Yes, I ... so."

4. *Each verb on the left goes together with two nouns on the right. Can you match them?*

a give
b invent
c design
d make
e form

1 ... an opinion
2 ... a house
3 ... an excuse
4 ... a command
5 ... a decision
6 ... an order
7 ... a story
8 ... a plan
9 ... a dress
10 ... a view

5. *Fill in the missing prepositions:* by, for, in, in, of, of, on, to

a) John has a good memory _____ names. b) The class had to learn the poem _____ heart. c) _____ my opinion, we shall win the match tomorrow. d) She reminds me _____ her mother. e) Tim is keen _____ football. f) Everything went according _____ plan. g) Please try to keep _____ mind what he wants. h) From my point _____ view no changes should be made.

ourselves and the others

communication (a)

45 the communication model · 46 facial expression, gesture · 47 voice

1. *What is he doing? He is ...*

2. *Gestures and what they mean: If you ... you might also say ...*

a	blush	1	"Come and look."
b	frown	2	"How right you are."
c	shake your head	3	"How stupid of me."
d	nod	4	"That's not the way I see it."
e	wave	5	"That's great."
f	shrug	6	"Just you try!"
g	shake your finger	7	"Oh dear."
h	beckon	8	"Sorry, no idea."
i	sniff	9	"Bye for now."
j	smile	10	"Oh, no! That's too bad."
k	stamp your feet	11	"Rubbish."

3. *Find one or two verbs that usually go together with the following.*

a) ... with pain; b) ... with fright; c) ... with rage; d) ... with laughter; e) ... for joy

4. *Choose the word that best fits the context.*

a) He ... (whistled / hummed) to his dog. b) He ... (groaned / gasped) with rage. c) He ... (muttered / murmured) a few angry words to himself. d) He ... (called / shouted) at the top of his voice.

5. *What may cause or lead ... ?*

a) a teacher to raise his voice; b) an old lady to call for help; c) a boy to shout with pain; d) an audience in a cinema to shriek with laughter; e) a young girl to weep bitterly; f) a man to whistle to his dog

communication (b)

45 the communication model · 48 say, speak · 49 write ·
50 correspondence · 51 read · 52 question, answer ·
53 affirmation, negation · 54 description · 55 narration · 56 exposition ·
57 argumentation · 58 instruction

1. *What are the things?*

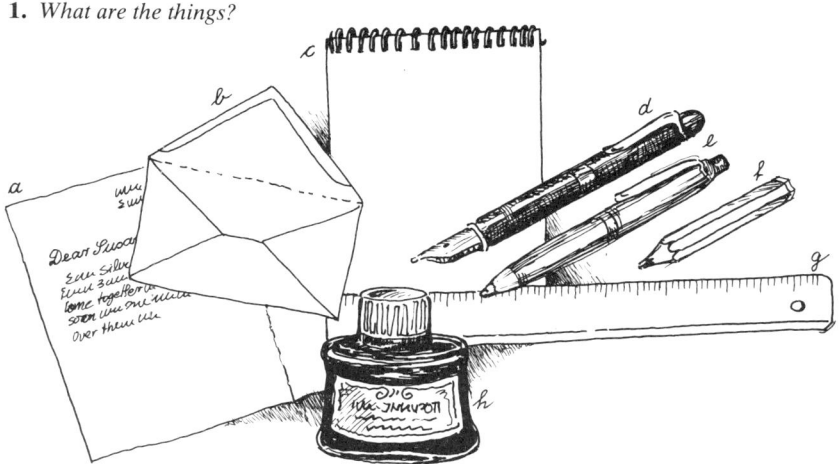

2. *Hidden words: Put a ring round the ten hidden verbs describing the use of language. Look in all directions of the grid.*

F	T	S	F	Q	K	V	X	Q	Q	U	L
I	N	S	T	R	U	C	T	I	S	M	C
N	Q	X	P	D	E	O	T	L	R	Q	C
C	E	W	V	T	E	I	P	T	T	O	R
I	V	N	I	O	U	S	Z	J	M	M	Y
E	C	R	I	H	O	M	C	M	D	N	W
X	W	S	H	F	Y	O	A	R	X	Y	T
P	Q	P	E	H	E	N	G	X	I	E	B
L	N	E	U	L	D	D	R	O	L	B	V
A	M	A	G	G	W	G	T	L	Q	R	E
I	Z	K	R	M	I	T	R	O	P	E	R
N	P	S	A	Y	X	H	A	P	K	N	E

26

3. *Rewrite the following anecdote, using the correct capital letters and punctuation marks.*

why not

there was a terrible fog Tim was driving home he could not see in the fog in front of him were two lights I will follow that car he said he followed it for half an hour suddenly he could not see the lights any more he drove on crash he had driven into the back of the car he had been following he jumped out of his car and was very angry why did you stop so suddenly and why did you switch off your lights why not said the old lady in the other car I am in my own garage

4. *Fill in the missing prepositions.*

a) She said "Good Morning" _____ us. b) Tom had a long talk _____ Mary. c) She writes all her letters _____ ink. d) I have corresponded _____ Tim for many years. e) He hasn't replied _____ my letter yet. f) Yes, I agree _____ you. g) He told us what happened _____ detail. h) What does the story deal _____? i) This sentence is an example _____ how to use the word "example".

5. *Which words often go together? Use each item only once.*

a	sign	1	... a conclusion
b	speak	2	... a speech
c	report	3	... good English
d	tell	4	... a message
e	make	5	... an argument
f	draw	6	... a problem
g	use	7	... a sign
h	explain	8	... an accident
i	deliver	9	... a comment
j	repeat	10	... a letter
k	send	11	... a poem
l	make	12	... a story

6. *Choose the word that best fits the context.*

a) He gave us an exact ... (report / description) of the house. b) Can you ... (explain / describe) to me how the engine works? c) We must ... (analyse / interpret) our present system before we try to improve it. d) Mother did not tell us about the ... (content / contents) of grandfather's letter. e) What are the ... (characterizations / characteristics) that distinguish the English from the French? f) Galilei ... (said / argued) that the earth was round. g) Have you any ... (proof / argument) that you were there at 8 o'clock? h) Try to ... (convince / persuade) him to come with us. i) The jury came to the ... (consequence / conclusion) that the accused was not guilty.

language

59 language · 60 word · 61 sentence, grammar · 62 style

1. *Find suitable words and put them in. Each dash stands for a letter.*

a) This was not quite _ _ _ _ _ _ _ _ . b) There was a small _ _ _ _ _ _ _ in what you said. c) Children learn foreign _ _ _ _ _ _ _ _ _ better than adults. d) It is useful for a boy or girl to learn _ _ _ _ _ _ _ languages, such as French and German. e) Children learn to _ _ _ _ _ _ before they learn to write. f) Heike's English is _ _ _ _ _ to understand. g) The Prime Minister's _ _ _ _ _ _ _ was printed in all the newspapers. h) A _ _ _ _ _ _ _ _ _ _ is a book which tells you what words mean. i) The English word "history" is _ _ _ _ _ _ _ from Latin. j) There was a mistake in your _ _ _ _ _ _ _ _ _ _ _ _ _ _ ; listen to how I say the word. k) In "The coffee is far too powerful" the word "powerful" does not _ _ _ _ in the context; the correct word is "strong".

2. *Choose the word that fits the context.*

a) The paper was written in very scientific ... (speech / language). b) It is by your ... (pronunciation / language) that I can tell that you are from Liverpool. c) I have studied ... (new / modern) languages. d) There are two ... (parts / syllables) in "belong". e) In what ... (sense / meaning) do you use this word? f) In the word "building" the ... (emphasis / stress) is on the first syllable. g) Many English words change their ... (spelling / writing) before the endings -ed, -es, and -ing. h) Most British and American English speakers can understand each other quite easily, though ... (pronunciation / pronouncement) can cause a few problems. i) "Cumulo-nimbus" is a scientific ... (terminus / term). j) Learning the finer points of English ... (usage / use) takes quite a long time.

3. *Explain how the following words change their meanings in the following collocations.*

a language: learn a language / use scientific language
b speech: make a speech / learn speech
c spell: "Please, spell your name." / Some children can't spell well

4. *Which words often go together? Use each item only once.*

a	know	1	... the first syllable
b	make	2	... a technical term
c	correct	3	... a language
d	look up	4	... with irony
e	spell	5	... an error
f	have	6	... a speech
g	stress	7	... a sentence
h	use	8	... your name
i	build	9	... a word in a dictionary
j	speak	10	... good pronunciation

5. *Which pairs of adjectives can be used in the expressions given below?*

a) spoken / written; b) good / poor; c) literal / figurative; d) small / capital; e) technical / scientific; f) rich / poor; g) simple / compound; h) clear / confused

1 have a ... vocabulary
2 use a word in a ... sense
3 write in a ... style
4 the ... language
5 speak ... English
6 a ... term
7 a ... sentence
8 begin with a ... letter

6. *What images are used in the following lines from a poem by W. H. Auden?*

> Here war is harmless like a monument:
> A telephone is talking to a man;
> Flags on a map declare that troops were sent;
> A boy brings milk in bowls ...

7. *Complete the sentences with suitable words.*

a The ... is the symbol of Christianity.
b Jerusalem is the symbol of ... .
c The ... reminds us of Jesus Christ.
d The Snake ... .
e The Light ... .

8. *Here are some conventional symbols used in literature. What does each stand for?*

a the voyage
b the ocean
c the traveller
d the night
e sleep

literature

63 stories · 64 drama · 65 poetry

1. *Hidden words: Put a ring round the ten hidden words describing different aspects of a literary work of art. The words are written in all directions.*

T	C	S	I	G	Q	V	S	Q	Y	U	H
C	H	A	R	A	C	T	E	R	O	N	M
S	Q	K	J	H	F	N	T	L	G	A	R
T	G	V	O	O	Y	I	P	I	W	R	M
A	N	C	Q	C	U	M	D	V	X	R	G
N	I	V	O	M	P	I	E	T	C	A	W
Z	T	X	H	Q	A	K	E	N	W	T	T
A	T	D	P	L	O	T	O	N	R	O	R
N	E	X	O	P	S	I	R	B	E	R	N
O	S	G	T	Y	T	N	F	R	Q	C	M
M	U	G	Z	C	L	P	T	L	X	Z	S
E	S	H	A	Y	Y	X	A	E	Q	H	I

Here is some help:
a) A ... in a story may be described as "round" or "flat". As a central ... he or she is also known as the "hero" or "heroine". b and c) When loosely applied, the two words we are looking for mean more or less the same: they refer to what happens in a story. More precisely, however, one of them is often described as placing emphasis on the cause and effect relationship of events in a story. d) We may say that the ... of "Lord of the Flies" is a South Sea island. e) Pupils must learn to distinguish between the author and the ... of a story. You should not confuse "Daniel Defoe" and "Robinson Crusoe". f and g) The next two words denote the divisions of a play. h) It is a written or spoken conversation in a book or play. i) We use the last two words to describe the form of a poem.

2. *Do you know the German titles of the following works?*

a G. Grass, The Tin Drum
b B. Brecht, The Threepenny Opera
c Th. Mann, Confessions of Felix Krull
d K. May, In the Desert
e F. Schiller, The Robbers
f H. Hesse, The Glass Bead Game
g E. M. Remarque, All Quiet on the Western Front
h G. Wallraff, Lowest of the Low

3. *Match the names of the ten English writers given below with the titles of their books.*
"... is the author of / wrote ..."

a	D. Defoe	1	Miss Marple's Final Case
b	J. Swift	2	Alice in Wonderland
c	M. Twain	3	Animal Farm
d	L. Carrol	4	Pygmalion
e	A. C. Doyle	5	Robinson Crusoe
f	A. Christie	6	Lord of the Flies
g	G. K. Chesterton	7	The Adventures of Tom Sawyer
h	G. Orwell	8	The Hound of the Baskervilles
i	W. Golding	9	Chips with Everything
j	G. B. Shaw	10	The Wisdom of Father Brown
k	A. Wesker	11	Rosencrantz and Guildenstern are dead
l	T. Stoppard	12	Gulliver's Travels

the mass media

66 the press · 67 radio, television · 68 film · 69 book

1. *Name the things shown in the pictures.*

2. *Word puzzle: Fill in the squares with words about the mass media.*

```
      T
      E
      L
      E
      V
      I
      S
      I
      O
      N
```

3. *Quiz*

a He is a well-known character in a strip cartoon in the *Daily Mirror*. He is a typical working class man and usually wears a flat cap.
b It is an affectionate name for the BBC. Literally it means "your father's or mother's sister".
c It is a popular daily radio programme telling of the life of a farming family. It has been broadcast since 1950. If you live in North Rhine-Westphalia or Lower Saxony and can tune in the BFBS, we are sure you know the name of the family, which is the name of the programme.
d It is the name of a street in central London where many national papers have their editorial offices. That's why it also means "the press" generally.
e It is a weekly humorous and satirical magazine. It was founded in 1841. When Bismarck, the German chancellor, resigned in 1890, it published a well-known cartoon ("Dropping the Pilot").
f It is the name of a daily popular paper. This paper is notorious for its sensational stories, and especially for its "page three", on which a nude female model appears every day.

4. *Explain how the meanings of the words change in the following sentences.*

a picture: Children like books with pictures. – We're going to the pictures tonight.
b shoot: Have you ever shot a deer? – This film was shot in California.
c volume: The volume of this container is 1,000 gallons. – We have a set of Shakespeare's works in 12 volumes.

5. *Match the pairs on the left with the expressions on the right. Use each item only once.*

a	serious / popular	1	the ... editor
b	front / back	2	a ... paper
c	news / city	3	the ... press
d	radio / TV	4	a ... film
e	documentary / silent	5	a ... programme
f	public / lending	6	the ... page
g	daily / Sunday	7	a ... library
h	news- / live	8	a ... station

6. *How are they different?*

a) bookshop and library; b) heading and headline; c) paperboy and newsagent; d) newspaper and magazine; e) news story and comment; f) advertisement and commercial; g) book and screenplay; h) printing office and printing-press; i) local paper and national paper; j) popular paper and quality paper

7. *Odd man out: Which word does not belong to the others? Why is it different?*

a heading – article – front page – column
b reporter – correspondent – editor – newsagent
c edition – circulation – issue – copy
d news story – comment – commercial – leader
e writer – printer – editor – correspondent
f viewer – listener – reader – commentator

our relations with others

70 alone, with others · 71 competition · 72 social position · 73 norm

1. *What are the words? Put in the missing vowels to find them.*

__l__n__; m____t; s__cc____d; f____l; p__w__r; __pp____nt;

__ff__c__; tr__d__t____n; r__l__

2. *Let's play charades: Put the pieces together again to find the words left out in the sentences below.*

am – bi – ca – cer – cess – chal – com – com – cus – e – er – ful – gath – ing – lenge – meet – mo – ny – ny – pa – pete – pres – reer – ri – suc – tige – tious – tom – val

a There will be a club ... tomorrow at 7.30 p.m.
b Many people ...ed in front of the hotel to see the famous pop star.
c She is very interesting and I enjoy her ...
d Will you ... in the 100 yards race?
e He is a very ... politician.
f I ...d him to a game of cards.
g No sport can ... rugby in excitement.
h He is a ... writer.
i A Rolls Royce may give you a lot of ...
j Tim chose a ... as a fireman.
k It is our ... to give presents at Christmas.
l The wedding ... is at 3 p.m.

3. *Match the words on the left with the expressions on the right. Use each item only once.*

a	friendly	1	a political ...
b	live	2	... a club
c	leave	3	... in an exam
d	together	4	... alone
e	meet	5	go for a walk ...
f	meeting	6	... to anything
g	join	7	on ... terms
h	company	8	... Tim alone
i	ambitious	9	have ... for dinner
j	rivals	10	have ... plans
k	successful	11	be old ...
l	yield	12	... in life
m	fail	13	... Tim in the street

4. *In each case find two adjectives that usually go together with the following.*

a) have ... power; b) have ... privileges; c) have ... status; d) have a(n) ... rank; e) have ... prestige

5. *Why do people ... ?*

a) obey rules; b) observe customs; c) advance rapidly in their careers; d) have high prestige with others; e) seek status; f) always give in to others; g) have no success; i) challenge other people; j) compete with others; k) keep others at a distance; l) lead a withdrawn life

6. *Which words can be derived from the following?*

meet; assemble; relation; compete; ambitious; rival; success; power; appoint; promote; custom; tradition

our family

74 courting, marriage · 75 family · 76 relatives

1. *A family tree is a table showing how the members of a family are related to one another. Study the family tree shown on p. 35 and fill in the missing words. Each dash stands for a letter.*

John is _ _ _ _ _ _ _ _ _ _ Pat. He is her _ _ _ _ _ _ _ and she is his _ _ _ _ _ _. They have three _ _ _ _ _ _ _ _ _, Timothy, Jane, and Maureen. John and Pat are their _ _ _ _ _ _ _ _. John is their _ _ _ _ _ _ _ and Pat is their _ _ _ _ _ _ _. Timothy is John's and

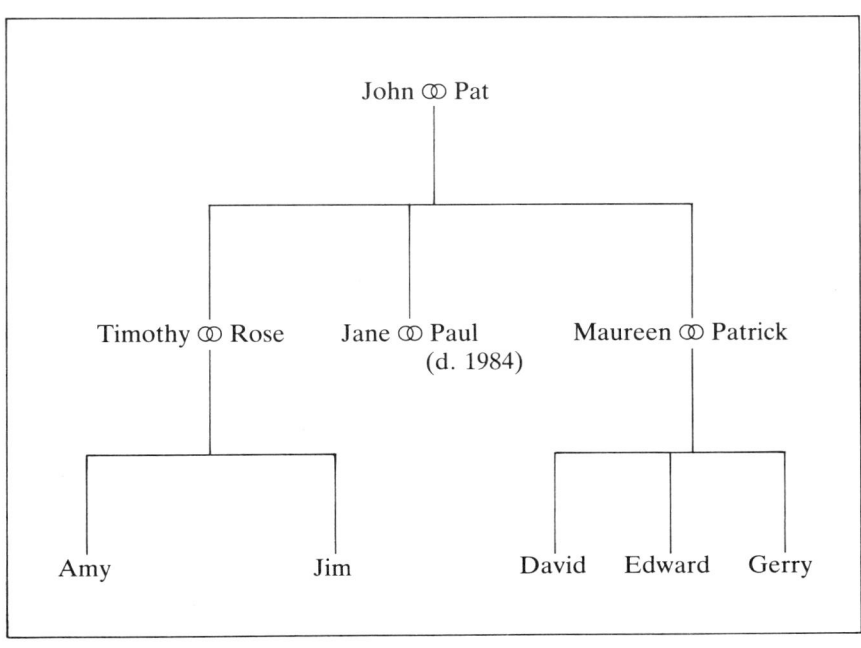

Pat's _ _ _ _, Jane and Maureen are their _ _ _ _ _ _ _ _ _ s. Amy has a _ _ _ _ _ _ _ _ _. She is Jim's _ _ _ _ _ _ _ _. John is Rose's and Patrick's _ _ _ _ _ _ _-_ _-_ _ _ _, Pat is their _ _ _ _ _ _ _-_ _-_ _ _. Timothy is David's, Edward's, and Gerry's _ _ _ _ _ _. They call him _ _ _ _ _ _ Timothy. Jane is the three boys' _ _ _ _ _ _, they call her "_ _ _ _ _ Jane". The three boys are Timothy's and Rose's _ _ _ _ _ _ _ _ s, Amy is Maureen's and Patrick's _ _ _ _ _ _. David and Edward were born on the same day. They are _ _ _ _ _ _. John is Amy's and Jim's _ _ _ _ _ _ _ _ _ _ _ _ _ _, Pat is their _ _ _ _ _ _-_ _ _ _ _ _ _. Amy is John's and Pat's _ _ _ _ _ _ _ _ _ _ _ _ _ _ _, Jim is their _ _ _ _ _ _ _ _ _. Patrick is Jane's _ _ _ _ _ _ _-_ _ _-_ _ _ _, she is his _ _ _ _ _ _ _-_ _-_ _ _ _. Jane's _ _ _ _ _ _ _ _ _ died in 1984. Since then she has been a _ _ _ _ _ _.

church

77 church building · 78 service · 79 faith

1. *Name the different buildings shown in the pictures.*

2. *Draw pictures of the following:*
bell; altar; candle; cross; organ; font

3. *What are the words? Fill in the missing letters to find them.*

a) The farmers are p _ _ _ ing that it will rain soon. b) The priest b _ _ _ _ ed the people before they left the church. c) We pray to G _ _ in church on Sundays. d) Jesus Christ died on the c _ _ _ _ _ . e) The Bible is the holy book of the C _ _ _ _ _ _ _ _ _ . f) They hope that at death their s _ _ _ goes to heaven. g) Satan is the name of the d _ _ _ _ . h) The little girl was c _ _ _ _ _ _ _ _ Mary.

4. *Match the words on the left with the expressions on the right.*

a	faith	1	praise ...
b	mass	2	St George, the patron ... of England
c	pray	3	sing a ...
d	hymn	4	... in God
e	heaven	5	sing in the church ...
f	penance	6	have ... in God
g	choir	7	say ...
h	gospel	8	a good ...
i	bless	9	... to God
j	Christian	10	preach the ...
k	believe	11	... the congregation
l	the Lord	12	do hard ... for your sins
m	Holy	13	go to ...
n	Ten	14	repent your ...
o	sins	15	the ... Commandments
p	saint	16	the ... Father

our school

80 school building · 81 staff · 82 time-table · 83 in class · 84 going to school, leaving school

1. *Hidden words: Put a ring round the ten subjects hidden in the grid. Look for them in all directions.*

H	V	P	K	G	Y	L	W	N	Q	K	I
K	F	Z	P	Z	R	N	A	M	R	E	G
P	G	G	B	U	O	M	Z	H	A	C	R
W	V	I	H	C	T	Q	K	M	D	V	B
C	H	E	M	I	S	T	R	Y	H	H	W
Z	P	F	H	S	I	L	G	N	E	O	H
Z	F	H	F	G	H	V	D	R	O	Q	X
Q	R	T	Y	H	Q	J	N	D	E	M	T
T	E	R	R	S	L	O	W	P	X	X	B
A	N	E	G	A	I	O	K	T	M	G	X
X	C	C	L	H	R	C	M	A	T	H	S
S	H	V	S	K	C	I	S	U	M	Q	U

2. *What are the things shown in the pictures?*

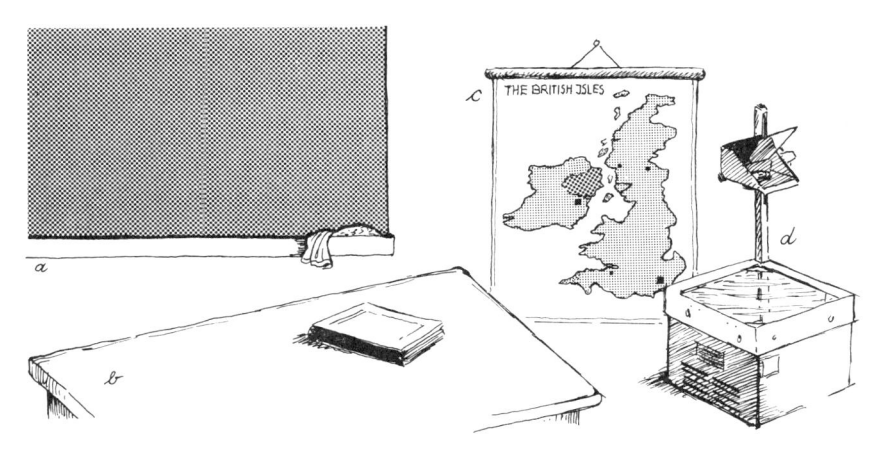

3. *Quiz: What are they?*

a) They are schools for children aged 5 to 11, after which they pass to a secondary school. b) They are large schools for children of all abilities. They provide a wide range of education. Today about 90% of all secondary school students attend this type of school. c) They are state or independent schools. They take pupils between 11 and 18. The name of this type of school comes from the fact that Latin grammar formed an important part of the teaching in former times. d) They are private, though their name makes you think of a state school. They are not only known for their high academic standard, but also – at least some people think so – for their exclusiveness and snobbery. e) In the U.K. it is a term used for some grammar schools for boys and in particular for many secondary schools for girls.

4. *Fill in the missing letters to find the words.*

a) Here's a piece of c _ _ _ _ _ . Now write on the b _ _ _ _ _ . b) Take out your b _ _ _ _ and open them at p _ _ _ 3. c) You were absent yesterday. Have you got a n _ _ _ ? d) For your h _ _ _ _ _ _ _ would you do exercise 3 on page 36. e) Who was a _ _ _ _ _ last time? f) C _ _ _ that from the board. g) Write an e _ _ _ _ on the following s _ _ _ _ _ _ : "The Daily Newspaper". h) How f _ _ did we get last time? If I remember correctly we were on page 16. i) Very good! There's nothing w _ _ _ _ with your answer. j) Please r _ _ _ _ _ lesson 5. There'll be a t _ _ _ on it sometime.

5. *When do you say this in the classroom?*

a) I'm sorry I didn't understand. b) Could you explain again, please? c) Why did you mark this wrong? d) I can't see. e) Why can't you say "I want that you should help me?" f) Where's the accent in this word? g) What's the meaning of "imagination"? h) What would be another way of saying it? i) Could I leave ten minutes early? j) I'm afraid I've left my book at home.

6. *Choose the word that best fits the context.*

a) My favourite ... (lesson / subject) is History. b) We have a ... (pause / break) from 10.00 to 10.20. c) After it we go back to our ... (classroom / class). d) Let's have a look at the ... (map / plan) of Europe. e) This exercise is to be done in your ... (textbooks / exercise books).

7. *Which words often go together? Use each item only once.*

a	clean	1	... an essay
b	fetch	2	... a test
c	mark	3	... the board
d	shut	4	... to school
e	do	5	... a map
f	write	6	... your books
g	get	7	... the register
h	pass	8	... an A in French
i	get	9	... to school
j	go	10	... an examination

our country (a)

85 constitution · 86 party · 87 election · 88 Parliament, Congress · 89 sitting · 90 government · 91 public finance · 92 foreign policy · 99 country

1. *Supply the missing vowels to find ten words used when talking about elections.*

c __ nd __ d __ t __ ; s __ __ t; pr __ gr __ mm __ ; c __ mp __ __ gn; p __ ll; b __ ll __ t; c __ nst __ t __ __ ncy; v __ t __ ; __ l __ ct; st __ nd f __ r

2. *Letter row: Underline the ten hidden words about government and parliament. They are written in this direction:* →

p a e t y a p a r t y i e s s a s e a s e a t s d a q y c j r d
e a r g s g d f e r v o t e o u t e r e l e c t i o n s o p s a
t i o n o p p o s i t i o n c e b e n b i n e t c a b i n e t c
a n g r e d e b a t e t e q c k b a t t e z a c t s w e r t m n
g d g o v e r n h s g d p r a s o t d e p a r t m e n t p t m n

3. *Fill in suitable words.*

a) English is not my ... language. b) We crossed the French-Spanish ... at Hendaye. c) Germany ... on Denmark in the north. d) If you lose your ... you can get a new one at the British Embassy. e) Nigeria declared its ... in 1960. f) The official name of West Germany is ... Republic of Germany. g) The U.K. is the short name of the United ... of Great Britain and Northern Ireland. h) Washington, D.C. is the ... of the U.S.A. i) The U.S. are sometimes called "God's own ... ". j) I am going ... for my holiday this year.

4. *Which words often go together? Use each item only once.*

a	stand for	1	... taxes
b	win	2	... the customs
c	fight	3	... a bill
d	hold	4	... a country
e	pass	5	... peace
f	govern	6	... an election
g	pay	7	... Parliament
h	hold	8	... a campaign
i	come to	9	... a treaty
j	conclude	10	... a conference
k	make	11	... a seat
l	get through	12	... an agreement

5. *How are they different?*

a) House of Commons and House of Lords; b) Senate and House of Representatives; c) front-bench MP and back-bench MP; d) cabinet and department; e) government and opposition; f) motion and debate; g) bill and act; h) safe seat and marginal seat; i) taxes and customs; j) kingdom and republic

6. *Fill in the correct prepositions, using the words given:* at, between, for, for, into, of, of, on, on, to, to, to, with

a) freedom _____ speech; b) the rights _____ man; c) sit _____ the throne; d) come _____ power; e) run _____ the Presidency; f) give your vote _____ a candidate; g) go _____ opposition; h) sit _____ a committee; i) be elected _____ a four-year term; j) the French ambassador _____ the U.S.; k) a treaty _____ two countries; l) be _____ peace _____ a country

our country (b)
93 the armed forces · 94 war

1. *What are the words? Fill in the missing letters to find them.*

a __ __ y; s __ l __ __ __ r; __ tt __ ck; __ i __ ht; d __ f __ nd; __ n __ m __ ;
b __ ttl __ ; g __ n; b __ m __ ; r __ fl __

2. *Find adjectives that can be used with the following.*

a) ... warfare; b) a(n) ... battle; c) in ... retreat; d) suffer ... defeat; e) demand ... surrender; f) ... weapons; g) ... ammunition; h) a(n) ... bomb; i) a(n) ... explosion; j) ... destruction

3. *Which words often go together? Use each item only once.*

    a join   1 ... a bridge
    b attack   2 ... a rifle / a shot
    c hit / miss   3 ... a battle
    d blow up / destroy   4 ... the army / the navy
    e win / lose   5 ... war
    f occupy   6 ... an attack
    g go to / declare   7 ... a country / a town
    h fire   8 ... a town / the enemy
    i fire / launch   9 ... a target
    j make / repel   10 ... a rocket

4. *Odd man out: Which does not belong to the others in the group?*

a attack – raid – advance – battle
b defeat – withdraw – flee – retreat
c occupy a town – seize a town – besiege a town – take a town
d bomb – gun – shell – grenade

our country (c)
95 crime · 96 police · 97 court · 98 prison

1. *Word scrabble: Find the missing words and fill the squares with them.*

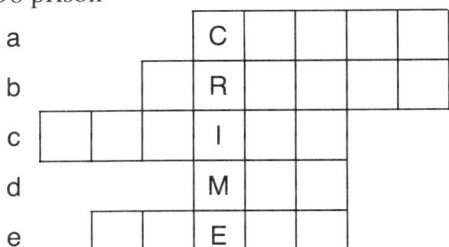

			C			
a						
b			R			
c			I			
d			M			
e			E			

2. *Which words often go together? Use each item only once.*

a	commit	1	... money
b	arrest	2	... a suspect
c	counterfeit	3	... a crime
d	rob	4	... in court
e	call	5	... a thief
f	inquire	6	... a case
g	question	7	... for murder
h	wanted	8	... the police
i	appear	9	... into a robbery
j	try	10	... a bank
k	accuse	11	... to prison
l	plead	12	... a witness
m	cross-examine	13	... a person of theft
n	pass	14	... guilty
o	go	15	... a sentence

3. *In each case add a word or phrase that usually goes with the given words.*

The police ...

... a burglar; ... a crime; ... investigations; ... for a wanted man; have a ... for a person's arrest; ... handcuffs on the arrested person; question a(n) ...

The accused ...

stands on ... for theft; is ... for stealing; pleads not ... to stealing; admits his ... ; is ... of theft; is ... to two years in prison; is ... for two years; makes a(n) ... to a higher court

The witness ...

is called in ... ; is under ... ; makes a(n) ... ; ... perjury

The prosecutor ...

brings a(n) ... of theft against a person; ... a person of theft; has enough ... to prove a person guilty

The jury ...

... a person guilty; returns a(n) ... of not guilty

The judge ...

... a person £250; ... a sentence of imprisonment; sentences a person to ten month's ... ; ... a person of robbery and orders his release

4. *Fill in the correct prepositions:* about, against, for, for, in, of, of, of, to, to

a) go _____ court; b) be sent to prison _____ murder; c) accuse a person _____ theft; d) rob an old woman _____ her purse; e) suspect a person _____ theft; f) be suspicious _____ a person; g) search _____ a wanted man; h) start a prosecution _____ a person; i) be _____ the dock; j) witness _____ the truth of sth

society

100 the social system · 101 class · 102 social group ·
103 population · 104 reform, revolution

1. *Fill in the missing vowels to find the words.*

organizat __ __ n; soc __ __ ty; bourg __ __ __ s __ __ ; p __ __ r; populat __ __ n; r __ __ t; upr __ __ r; rev __ l __ t __ __ n; ref __ g __ __ ; assoc __ __ tion

2. *What are the words?*

a) S... has changed a lot in the last hundred years. b) Working c... people are usually poorer than middle c... people. c) I am going on holiday with a g... of friends. d) I belong to a tennis c... and play every Wednesday. e) London has a p... of ten million. f) There was a big c... at the football match. g) UNESCO is the short name for United Nations Educational, Scientific, and Cultural O.... h) Millions of i... came from Europe to America. i) The great economic and social change that started in Britain in the second half of the 18th century is called the Industrial ... .

3. *Put in the missing prepositions.*

a) live _____ society; b) a group _____ sb's leadership;
c) crowd _____ a room; d) emigrate _____ a country;
e) immigrate _____ a country; f) drive the population _____ revolt; g) rise _____ the government; h) be _____ noble rank;
i) call _____ reforms

our working life

work (a)

105 employment · 107 income · 108 trade union, strike

1. *What are the words? Fill in the missing letters to find them.*

a) w __ rk; b) __ mpl __ __ ; c) __ nc __ m __ ; d) __ __ rn; e) tr __ d __ __ n __ __ n; f) str __ k __ ; g) __ n __ mpl __ y __ d; h) __ ppl __ c __ t __ __ n; i) l __ b __ __ r; j) d __ sm __ ss

2. *Which words often go together? Use each item only once.*

a	write	1	... work
b	employ	2	... a trade union
c	find	3	... a strike
d	work	4	... low wages
e	call	5	... a good wage
f	join	6	... notice to an employee
g	get	7	... an application
h	pay	8	... overtime
i	give	9	... a pension
j	earn	10	... fifty men

3. *Replace the words in ( ) to get the opposite meaning.*

a) pay (high) wages; b) have a (poor) income; c) a (poor) man; d) come from a (well-to-do) family; e) live in (luxury); f) be (in) employment; g) a (good) workman

4. *Fill in the correct prepositions:* at, for, for, in, in, on, on, on, of, of

a) apply _____ a job; b) work _____ an office; c) be _____ overtime; d) employ a staff _____ 20; e) live _____ a small income; f) live _____ poverty; g) be _____ strike; h) strike _____ better pay; i) retire _____ the age of 60; j) be out _____ employment

5. *Which derivatives and compounds can you make from the following?*
a) employ; b) work; c) labour; d) wealth; e) strike

6. *Here are some English proverbs. Invent situations in which a speaker may use them.*

a) A bad workman always blames his tools. b) All work and no play makes Jack a dull boy. c) Give us the tools and we'll finish the job. d) The labourer is worthy of his hire. e) A Jack of all trades is master of none. f) Too many cooks spoil the broth. g) Many hands make light work.

work (b)

106 occupations

1. *Change the order of the letters to find the words for occupations.*

a) rerfma; b) ocok; c) litop; d) polainecm; e) lecetirinac; f) dootrc; g) psntamo; h) hcmeicna; i) ecrseyrat; j) usrdberiv

2. *Guess my job.*

a) A member of the class comes to the front and makes movements typical of a certain job (like moving fingers as if typewriting). The rest of the class try to guess.
b) A member of the class comes to the front and thinks of a job. The rest of the class try to guess what his or her job is. The pupil at the front answers questions – up to 20 – but he or she only answers: "Yes, I am/have/do." or: "No, I'm not/haven't/don't." You may ask questions like "Do you need a(n) ... to do your work?" or: "Do you work in a(n) ... ?" or "Are you a(n) ... ?"

3. *In a careers office: Complete these short dialogues with the items given below. Practise with a partner.*

– Careers officer: "What would you like to do?"
– Applicant: "I'd like to ... "
– Careers officer: "Then you could be a(n) ..."

a) put together machines or electrical parts; b) look after sick people; c) repair cars; d) plan houses; e) load and unload ships; f) work on a ship; g) fit and repair water pipes and bathroom articles; h) write articles for a newspaper; i) sell flowers; j) drive lorries

– Careers officer: "Where would you like to work?"
– Applicant: "I'd like to work ... "
– Careers officer: "Then you could be a(n) ..."

a) in a hospital; b) on the railway; c) on a building site; d) in an office; e) at a garage; f) in a shop; g) in a bank; h) at a coalmine; i) in a bookshop; j) at the customs

4. *Tell the class what job each person in the list does.*

a) dressmaker; b) farmer; c) hairdresser; d) pilot; e) captain; f) journalist; g) actor; h) dentist; i) forester; j) butcher

5. *Match the AE words on the left with their BE equivalents on the right.*

    a longshoreman   1 chemist
    b engineer   2 lawyer
    c truck driver   3 docker
    d mailman   4 shop assistant
    e pharmacist   5 lorry driver
    f sales clerk   6 shop keeper
    g store-keeper   7 engine driver
    h attorney   8 postman

6. *Change the order of the jobs in the list below. Begin with the job you think is most important. Which is the second, third, ... least important in your opinion?*

actor – baker – banker – bricklayer – doctor – farmhand – football player – hairdresser – pilot – policeman – teacher

production

109 power, energy · 110 manufacturing, tools · 111 factory · 112 farm

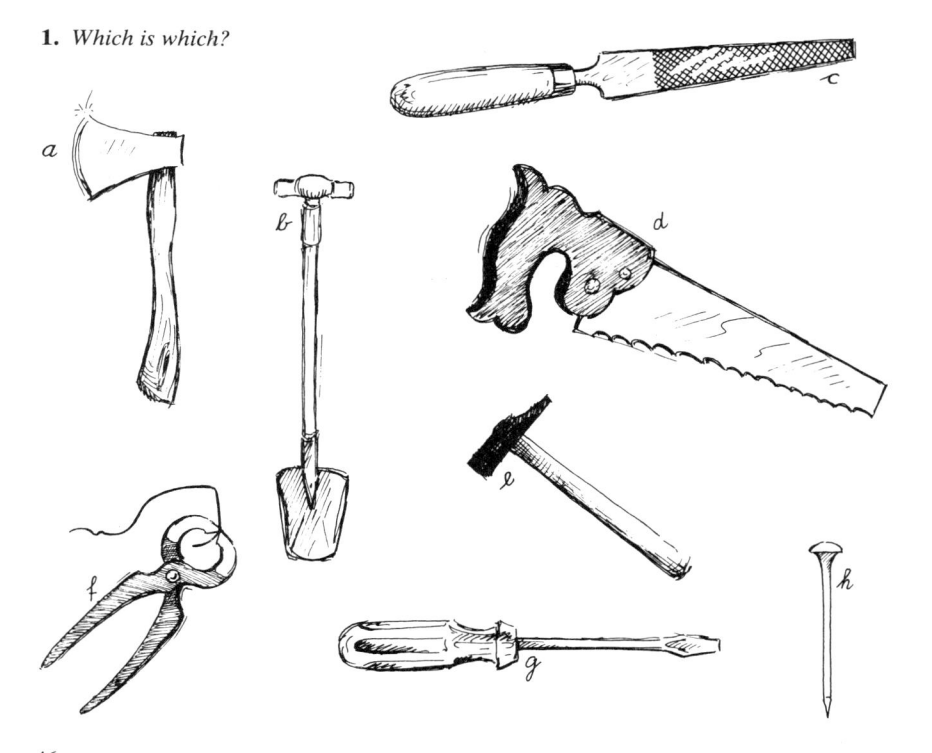

1. *Which is which?*

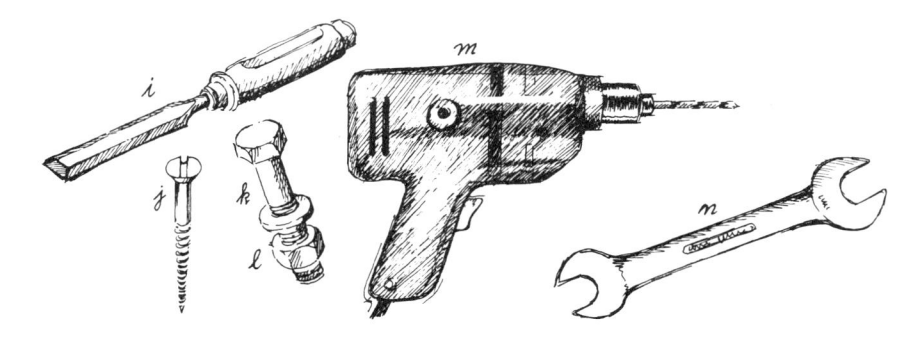

2. *Complete the sentences by adding a suitable word.*

a) The wheel is turned by water p.... b) My car has a small e...; it can't go very fast. c) Many f... workers belong to a trade union. d) He's making a table in the w... behind the house. e) Have you got a t... for taking the wheels off a car? f) If John works o... he doesn't come home before seven. g) The night s... in the factory starts at 10 p.m. h) Many factories have an a... line and the article is built up as it goes from one person to another along the line. i) When the factory w... blows all the workers c... out and make their way home.

3. *Which words often go together? Use each item only once.*

a	save	1	a chemical ...
b	coal	2	a steam ...
c	electric	3	be on ...
d	plant	4	work in a ... mine
e	textile	5	a ... farm
f	engine	6	... energy
g	shift	7	the ... industry
h	overtime	8	... the production
i	cattle	9	generate ... power
j	increase	10	work on the night ...

4. *Which word fits the context best?*

a) He is making a chair in the ... (factory / workshop) behind the house. b) Mr Jones is an ... (electrical / electric) engineer. c) The country does not ... (produce / manufacture) enough oil. d) Many goods formerly made by hand are now made on ... (machines / engines). e) Thousands of people are employed in the ... (making / manufacture) of shoes. f) Cows are milked by hand or by ... (electric / electrical) machines. g) The people who ... (assemble / build) cars have to work very quickly.

5. *What are the words?*

a) a very large farm in the western U.S. where cattle, sheep or horses are produced: ...; b) a building for keeping animals, esp. horses: ... ; c) a person that works on a farm: ... ; d) a building on a farm in which the farm equipment is kept: ...

trade

113 buying, selling · 114 shop · 115 goods · 116 price

1. *Find the missing words and fill the empty squares with them.*

a			S					
b			H					
c			O					
d			P					
e			P					
f			I					
g			N					
h			G					

Here is some help:
a "How's ...?"
b I buy my food at the ... on the corner.
c The AE word for "shop".
d The ... of gold is forbidden in many countries.
e The owner of a small shop.
f Many car dealers allow a ... of 3% if you pay cash.
g Fish and fruit are some of the products that are often sold in ... .
h A ... sells sugar, salt, tea, rice, flour and many other things for the house.

2. *Fill in the missing words.*

Mrs Brown goes shopping

Mrs Brown went to the shopping centre to have a look at things, not to buy them. She just wanted to go ... . But suddenly she saw some lovely blouses. She went into the shop and asked how much they were. The assistant said: "The regular price is £30 but now they're only £8 each. We're selling them ... at ... prices." After a long time she decided to take the fantastic green blouse. At home she told her husband: "I got this at a ... . I've made a ... , you know." Her husband said: "You look sick in a green blouse." The next day Mrs Brown said to the assistant: "I want to ... this blouse. Have you got a red one?" But the assistant said: "I'm sorry. We've got no more reduced blouses. We're ... of them." Poor Mrs Brown!

3. *What is Mrs Miller putting into her shopping trolley?*

a) one ten-pound ... of potatoes; b) one ... of jam; c) a ... of chocolate; d) three ... of wine; e) two ... of eggs; f) ten ... of matches; g) a ... of bananas; h) one ... of beer; i) three ... of fish; j) four ... of cigarettes

4. *What is the difference between ...?*

a) a department store and a supermarket; b) a shop and a shopping precinct; c) a product and some produce; d) an offer and an order; e) a shopping-trolley and a shopping basket; f) a cash-register and a cash desk

5. *What has Mr Jones asked?*

a Mr Jones: ... ? – It's 65p, sir.
b Mr Jones: ... ? – Oh, they're £2.50 each.
c Mr Jones: ... ? – The price will be something like £40, but I'll ask the manager.
d Mr Jones: ... ? – Oh, yes, certainly. But we'll allow 3% discount for cash payment.

6. *Fill in the word that best fits the context:* price, cost, fees, expenses

a) He sold his house at a good ... . b) I've calculated the ... of having the house painted and I think we can afford it. c) What's the ... of this book? d) He sold his stamp collection at a ... much below its real value because he needed the money. e) He hasn't yet paid the ... for his French course at the language school. f) He couldn't save any money because of his ... . g) The ... of living in big cities is much higher than in small towns. h) In England you needn't pay a doctor's ... if you go to the National Health Service.

money

117 currency · 118 banking, insurance, stock exchange ·
119 spend money, owe money

1. *What are the words? Put in the missing letters to find them.*

a) m __ n __ __ __ ; b) c __ __ __ n; c) p __ nn __ ; d) p __ __ nd; e) d __ ll __ r;

f) c __ nt; g) n __ ck __ l; h) d __ m __ ; i) q __ __ rt __ r

2. *Say how much it is.*

a) It's 85p. b) It's £7. c) It's £2.45. d) It's $1.50. e) It's 78c. f) It's $2.45.

3. *Rewrite the sentences in different words.*

a) Could you lend me $200? – Can I ... $200 from you? b) I lent you £50. – You ... £50 from me. c) Don't waste! – ...! d) Why are you spending all the money your uncle has left you? – Why don't you ... ? e) I've no money in my account. – My account is ... . f) I got my bank to pay me more money than I had in my account. – I ... my account. g) As I had no cash about me, I paid by cheque. – I ... a cheque. h) I have to pay $180 on a loan of $2,000. – I had to pay 9% ... .

4. *Match the words on the left with the expressions on the right. Use each item only once.*

a	borrow	1	... cheque
b	save	2	... your friend £10
c	lend	3	... a new car every two years
d	owe	4	... £50 from your account
e	pay in	5	... money from a bank
f	draw	6	... £100 to your account
g	pay by	7	... £2 each week
h	hold	8	... £1,000 for a new computer
i	afford	9	... your friend £5 till Monday
j	spend	10	... shares in a company

5. *What would you do in these situations?*

a Having just read in the FINANCIAL TIMES that the computer industry is still expanding rapidly, you think of the £5,000 in your bank you do not need at the moment.
b In a London antique-shop you see the chair you've been looking for for ages. Unfortunately, however, you've no cash on you.
c Your car is six years old and you're thinking of buying a new one, but you've only £1,500 in your account.
d You need £500 for four weeks, but your account is empty.
e Your Uncle George has left you 100 shares worth about $150 each. You want to buy a new house and need money.

6. *Put in the right prepositions.*

a Can I pay you tomorrow? I've no cash ... me.
b The bill amounts ... £125.
c I spent £5,000 ... a new car.
d I'm short ... money this week. Can you lend me some?
e His credit is good ... $10,000.
f You're ... debt to me for $200.

our leisure time

holidays

120 holiday · 121 travelling · 122 hotel · 123 camping

1. *Letter grid: Put a ring round the ten words about holidays and travelling. Look for them in all directions.*

H	P	T	C	G	O	U	S	Q	W	Q	Q
T	O	U	R	I	S	T	G	X	X	L	B
P	Y	K	N	A	L	Q	I	A	D	C	R
T	R	I	P	T	V	E	R	P	X	A	W
T	N	M	R	T	S	E	T	Q	X	M	G
T	E	V	N	C	P	W	L	O	Y	P	Y
O	I	W	U	F	E	H	M	F	H	I	A
V	V	O	T	E	K	C	I	T	T	N	D
T	N	H	K	R	M	Y	X	R	V	G	I
G	E	E	C	A	R	A	V	A	N	I	L
O	N	N	Z	M	L	O	I	L	J	M	O
D	S	Z	T	S	Y	Q	K	C	Q	H	H

2. *Draw pictures to show how they are different.*

a) bag and suitcase; b) tent and caravan; c) sleeping bag and rucksack; d) single room and double room

3. *Which words on the left often go together with the pairs on the right. Use each item only once.*

    a book   1 ... sightseeing / camping
    b carry   2 ... by train / by air
    c go   3 ... a journey / a trip
    d make   4 ..: a ticket / a guide
    e buy   5 ... a flight / a room
    f travel   6 ... a suitcase / a bag

4. *Find nouns that often go together with the following.*

a travel by ...   b stay at a ...   c go on ...
d go on a ...   e leave the key at the ...   f be on ...

5. *Choose the word that best fits the context.*

a) It was a sunny day and we made a nice ... (trip / voyage) on the Thames. b) Where's your hand ... (luggage / package)? c) Many ... (tourists / sightseers) go to France every year. d) We're going on a ... (tour / trip) of London this afternoon. e) I've booked a double room with a ... (bathroom / bath). f) When checking in at a hotel you often have to sign the ... (reception / register). g) I went to the ... (travel agency / tourist information) to book a flight to London.

6. *Word building: Find as many new words as you can by combining the 19 words listed below. The new words are written as two words.*

bag – camping – check – class – hand – holidays – leisure – luggage – package – room – school – sightseeing – single – site – sleeping – time – tour – tourist – traveller's

7. *Put in the right prepositions.*

a) Where are you going _____ your holidays? b) He had a lot of luggage _____ him. c) Last year I travelled _____ Spain through France. d) We're going _____ a trip to Brighton _____ the day. e) I bought a guide for visitors _____ Britain. f) We stayed _____ a nice and comfortable hotel. g) We camped _____ the night _____ a little brook. h) The ground was so hard that we had to hammer the pegs _____ it.

sports and games

124 sport · 125 games, sports · 126 football, soccer

1. *How are they different?*

a long jump and high jump
b skating and roller-skating
c boxing and wrestling
d throwing the discus and throwing the javelin
e weight lifting and shot put

2. *In which form of sport is the person illustrated partaking?*

3. *What kinds of sport do you need these things for?*

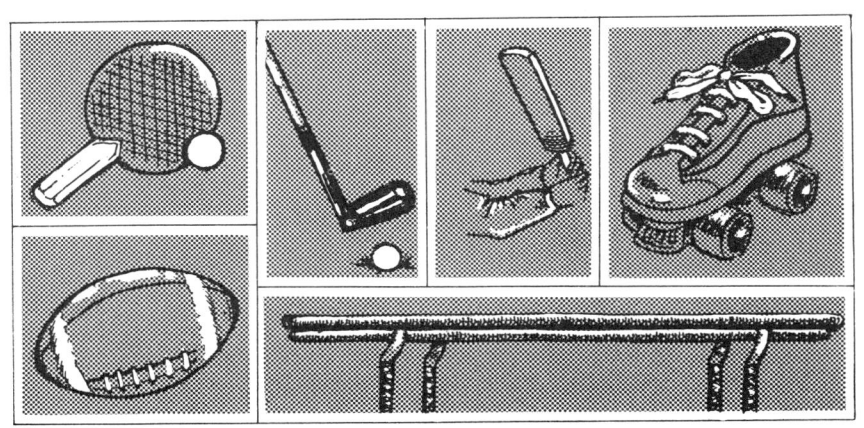

4. *Fill in the empty squares with words about sports and games.*

5. *Match the words in the left column with the expressions in the right column. Find as many pairs as possible.*

a	win	1	... a goal
b	lose	2	... in a race
c	compete	3	... coach
d	score	4	... jump
e	break	5	... a game
f	football	6	... the cup
g	long	7	... by 1 goal to 2
h	foul	8	... a point
i	free	9	... a match
j	halfway	10	... match
k	out of	11	... the championship
l	cup	12	... in a championship
m	end	13	... the world record
		14	... by 2 goals to 1
		15	... a race
		16	... in a tournament
		17	... shape
		18	... final
		19	... in a draw
		20	... form
		21	... line
		22	... kick
		23	... play

6. *Choose the word that best fits the context.*

a) Soccer is a ... (match / game) for two teams. b) There is a football ... (match / game) this afternoon. c) Every morning John spends two hours ... (practising / training) for the race.

7. *The narrator is reporting a sporting event on the radio. What form of sport is he describing?*

a "There is now a light wind blowing across the links. After a long drive of 180 yards, Jack Thompson is trying for a birdie on the eighth hole."
b "It is a beautiful morning here on the bank of the Thames. The members of the Oxford crew are already in their boat, but the Cambridge team is still not finished."
c "The snow on the slopes is sparkling in the spring sun. And here comes the Swedish champion towards the finishing line at a tremendous speed."
d "O'Mally gives Mohammed a left hook. Mohammed reacts with several hard punches to O'Mally's head ... and he's down ... the referee is counting ..."
e "And now the moment the whole world has been waiting for. Michail Nobodnik, the Russian Giant, will attempt to break the world record. Will he be able to get 498 lbs. off the floor?"
f "It's a fascinating duel here on the centre court. Becker is serving. Mecir returns the ball with a beautiful backhand. Becker's moved to the net – a shot like a rocket. No hope for Mecir now."
g "A pass by Johnson to the left, and now forward to McGuire, number 18. Manchester's Smith moves in to take the ball, but the referee calls a foul and gives Liverpool a free kick."

art and entertainment

127 music · 128 dancing · 129 theatre · 130 painting, drawing, sculpture · 131 photography · 132 circus, fun fair, variety show

1. *Syllable scrabble: Find the words for six musical instruments by putting the pieces together again.*

clar – gui – i – lin – net – no – o – o – pet – phone – pia – sax – tar – trum – vi

2. *Which words often go together? Use each item only once.*

a sing
b play
c put on
d perform
e paint
f draw
g carve
h shape
i take
j juggle

1 ... a record
2 ... a statue out of wood
3 ... a picture
4 ... the piano
5 ... a photo
6 ... balls
7 ... clay into a pot
8 ... a song
9 ... a play
10 ... a cartoon

3. *Choose the word that best fits the context.*

a) My daughter sings in the church ... (chorus / choir). b) This statue has been ... (carved / formed) from stone. c) Bob made a pencil ... (painting / drawing) of a man on a horse. d) Picasso was a Spanish ... (artiste / artist). e) I hung a picture of Tower Bridge ... (on / at) the wall to make it look nicer. f) This song is arranged for three ... (singers / voices). g) The first act has three ... (parts / scenes). h) There is ... (a presentation / an exhibition) of modern paintings at the picture gallery. i) I'd like to have two ... (prints / pictures) each from these negatives. j) The ... (clown / magician) produced a rabbit from his hat.

4. *Choose adjectives from the following list to complete the expressions below.*

deep – exact – famous – flattering – good – interesting – large – lifelike – modern – popular – shocking – small – successful – wooden

a) keep ... time; b) have a(n) ... voice; c) sing a(n) ... song; d) a(n) ... production of a play; e) a(n) ... audience; f) an exhibition of ... art; g) a(n) ... painter; h) a(n)... portrait; i) a(n) ... frame

5. *What makes people go to ... ?*

a) a museum; b) a concert; c) the theatre; d) a circus

6. *Word building: Put a word from the first group with one from the second group. The new expressions are written as two words.*

band – cassette – colour – dancing – fun – hit – lion – pop
fair – film – leader – music – parade – recorder – school – tamer

7. *Put in the right prepositions.*

a) a song composed _____ C major; b) play a record _____ the Beatles; c) put _____ a record; d) paint _____ water-colours; e) make two prints _____ the negative; f) do stunts _____ the trapeze; g) ride _____ a merry-go-round; h) sing a song _____ the guitar; i) go _____ a ball; j) be _____ stage; k) sit _____ a portrait

the world around us

our home (a)

133 building a house · 134 owner, tenant · 135 live ·
136 house · 137 room

1. *Name the houses shown in the pictures.*

2. *Letter row: Put a line under the ten words for parts of a house. The words are written like this:* →

s g d f e r t e u d o o r h d g p b e l l e l l a l q w e r a t
o d z w h a l l f s g e t z u a s t a i r s g s f e j y x s a w
r h s z e o p f l o o r a f f s a r o o f m n x y b c v d f g s
s t o r x s t o r e y f s d w a w e l l w a l l o p e r i k a j
h d g c b y m r o o m f s d e r a a w i n d o w d s f e r t w z

57

3. *Draw pictures to show how the following are different.*

a) brick and tile; b) fence and wall; c) gate and door; d) step and stairs; e) floor and ceiling; f) bath and shower; g) chair and armchair; h) carpet and curtain; i) lamp and candle

4. *Which words often go together? Use each item only once.*

a	build	1	... the bell
b	ring	2	... the curtains
c	pay	3	... the stairs
d	go up	4	... the window
e	take	5	... the door
f	draw	6	... a house
g	turn on	7	... the lift
h	open	8	... the key
i	turn	9	... rent
j	shut	10	... a lamp

5. *Find seven new words by combining the 14 words listed below. The new words are written as one word.*

bell – brick – case – door – gate – layer – light – paper – spot – stair – stairs – up – wall – way

our home (b)

138 bedroom, rest · 139 bathroom, hygiene · 140 kitchen, housework · 141 dining-room · 142 study · 143 sitting-room · 144 nursery

1. *Letter grid: Find the ten words for pieces of furniture. Look for the words in all directions.*

L	T	I	F	Y	Q	M	X	N	I	L	E
C	U	P	B	O	A	R	D	P	S	N	C
O	P	G	R	O	F	S	H	W	G	A	A
T	R	V	O	L	O	U	Q	L	Q	R	R
W	X	I	E	O	T	K	Z	N	M	S	R
A	C	H	A	H	P	X	C	C	Y	O	V
R	S	O	O	H	X	K	H	A	W	F	X
D	Q	D	E	V	C	A	G	J	S	A	R
R	W	Y	L	M	I	T	Q	M	B	E	V
O	M	M	B	R	Q	Y	I	H	Z	T	Q
B	E	D	A	K	T	E	N	I	B	A	C
E	G	S	T	R	H	F	U	P	N	I	C

2. *Draw pictures to show how they are different.*

a) wardrobe and bookcase; b) pillow and cushion; c) bed and sofa; d) chair and armchair; e) cupboard and bookshelf; f) pot and pan; g) cup and saucer; h) brush and broom

3. *Here are some words with mixed-up letters for things that you can find in the kitchen. Put them in the right order again.*

onops – otp – cersau – puc – tyra – bleat – rkof – lowb – guj – ikfne

4. *Find words to fit the following definitions or descriptions.*

a) a woollen cloth we put on the bed to keep warm: ... ; b) It wakes you by making a loud noise in the morning: ... ; c) You use it when you brush your teeth: ... ; d) to cut the hair from the face: ... ; e) It is in the kitchen; you can cook on it: ... ; f) It is in the kitchen, too; you keep milk and butter and other things in it to keep them fresh and cold: ... ; g) This word means "knives, forks, spoons": ... ; h) You can keep books on it, but not only books; when it is in the kitchen, plates are kept in it: ...

5. *Housework: Which words often go together? Use each item only once.*

a	make	1	... the sitting-room
b	lay	2	... the baby
c	dust	3	... the bed
d	clean	4	... the dishes
e	sweep	5	... the table
f	bath	6	... the hoover
g	wash	7	... the furniture
h	wipe	8	... the garden path
i	tidy	9	... the windows
j	use	10	... the floor

6. *Fill in the right prepositions.*

a) sit _____ a sofa / _____ an armchair / _____ a table;

b) lie _____ bed / _____ the couch

our town, our village

145 town, village · 146 buildings and places · 147 street · 148 services · 149 post office · 150 restaurant

1. *Name the things shown in the picture.*

2. *Hidden words: Put a ring round the ten hidden words for buildings and places in a town. Look for them in all directions.*

B	D	X	V	R	L	C	H	X	D	F	V
A	Y	M	O	O	M	O	O	I	S	U	E
H	O	S	P	I	T	A	L	F	C	X	P
K	T	P	J	E	S	A	G	H	V	T	U
C	G	U	L	M	N	A	Z	P	M	H	D
L	E	B	E	R	T	A	E	H	T	Y	X
O	S	M	X	L	T	S	B	F	C	S	A
U	L	U	E	I	O	O	Z	H	U	M	N
C	T	S	T	T	T	O	U	T	E	M	Q
K	S	E	B	L	E	R	H	N	T	H	N
X	J	U	Z	R	C	R	I	C	J	E	A
N	Q	M	G	H	D	C	Y	Y	S	J	D

3. *Complete the following description.*

A tour of London

London is a very busy c... , with many famous s...s. Walking down Whitehall, we are in one of the most famous s...s of the world. It runs from Trafalgar Square to the Houses of Parliament and contains many important b...s and government offices. Pall Mall is noted for its many clubs. From St. James's Park it's only a short walk to Westminster Abbey, a c... in Westminster, where almost all the English sovereigns have been crowned since the 11th century. The British M... contains one of the world's largest collections of antiquities. It is so full of interesting things that you have never enough time to see everything you want. What could be better than a day at the Z... in Regent's P.... It is Britain's best-known zoological garden and was opened in 1826.

4. *Word building: Find as many new words as you can by combining the 26 words listed below.*

box – brigade – bus – crossing – fire – hall – hour – jam – lights – market – office – police – pool – post – railway – rush – square – station – station – stop – swimming – telephone – town – traffic – traffic – zebra

5. *Try to explain how they are different.*

a) village and town; b) swimming bath and swimming pool; c) crossroads and level crossing; d) signpost and road sign; e) library and museum; f) airport and harbour; g) hotel and restaurant; h) snack bar and pub

6. *Fill in the right prepositions.*

a live _____ 49, Greencroft Road, London SE 1

b walk _____ the pavement

c take the first turning _____ the left

d a lot of traffic _____ the roads

e _____ the rush hour

f go _____ town

g walk _____ the road

h follow the signposts _____ Thorpe-le-Soken

i work _____ the City

j park _____ a parking metre

k live _____ a small village

transport

151 by bicycle, by motor-cycle · 152 by car · 153 road · 154 by bus, by underground · 155 by train · 156 by plane · 157 by ship

1. *Name the things shown in the pictures.*

2. *Complete the following words for motor vehicles and their parts.*

a) v __ n; b) l __ __ ry; c) __ ng __ n __ ; d) bo __ __ __ __ t; e) cl __ t __ h;

f) __ yr __ ; g) __ oo __ ; h) k __ y; i) c __ ac __

3. *Let's do charades: Find eleven words about trains and planes by putting the pieces together again.*

air – cab – com – con – duc – en – ger – gine – in – lot – ment – part – pas – pi – port – rail – run – sen – sta – table – time – tion – tor – way – way

4. *Rearrange the letters to find words connected with ships and harbours.*

baadro – isal – ticapan – oahurbr – aldo – ortp – lsraio – yrrfe – cdek – binac

5. *Which words often go together? Use each item only once.*

a	go	1	... a car
b	start	2	... the bus
c	drive	3	... the seat belts
d	check	4	... by ship
e	take	5	... a cabin
f	buy	6	... by bike
g	fasten	7	... a plane
h	fly	8	... a ticket
i	travel	9	... the engine
j	book	10	... the oil

6. *Which word fits the context?*

a) Yesterday I ... (rode / drove) 200 miles on my new motorbike. b) It costs 25p an hour to park in this ... (car park / park place). c) Every morning I go to town ... (with the / by) bus. d) Only few people were waiting at the bus ... (station / stop). e) There is a bridge where the road crosses the ... (train / railway). f) "Passengers for Edinburgh please go to ... (Gate / Door) 12." g) The plane ... (took off / started) from Heathrow at 0800 hours. h) The ship ... (sails / goes) to London tomorrow. i) This morning we are going on a ... (coach / bus) tour of London.

7. *Fill in the right prepositions.*

a) go _____ car; b) ride _____ a car; c) leave the car _____ the car park; d) come _____ a crossroads; e) wait _____ the bus stop; f) meet a friend _____ the station; g) take the 10.00 train _____ London; h) change _____ Colchester _____ Ipswich; i) go _____ ship; j) lie _____ harbour; k) lie _____ anchor

animals around us

158 animals in the house · 159 animals on the farm · 160 animals in the fields and forests · 161 animals in or near the water · 162 animals in the zoo · 163 man and animals · 164 the sounds of animals · 165 the animal

1. *Letter row: Underline the ten hidden words for animals that live in the house or on the farm. The words are written like this: → or like this: ←.*

a h s g d t g o d j d e g a h d g f a h e e p p t a c l h m b j
g h k s x o h d g j s s h e a p p e g i p r t z r u a j g s f d
g s h e e p o w c f s g d f p o e c h s s h h a s w o c d s i p
q w e r t z h o r s e u i a s y x c v b n d f h h e n a s d f g
h j k k s h t a o g m s t e r w a s d n e m x d b u d g i e e a

2. *Complete the following words for animals in the zoo.*

__ io __ ; t __ __ er; __ ea __ ; __ l __ p __ a __ t; c __ m __ __ ; ch __ m __ ;
__ e __ p __ r __ ; an __ __ l __ p __ ; __ eb __ a; __ ro __ __ di __ __

3. *Name the animals shown in the pictures.*

4. *Put in the missing words.*

a We have hair. A fox has .... A bird has ...s.
b We have hands. A cat has .... A bird has ....
c We have a mouth. A bird has a ... or a bill. A penguin has a ... too.
d We have fingers. A horse has ....
e A fish has fins. A dolphin and a whale have ....

5. *The voices of animals.*

Which animals ... ?

a) bark; b) mew and purr; c) moo; d) crow; e) sing; f) roar; g) trumpet; h) neigh; i) hum; j) grunt

Which sounds are made by the following animals?

a) frogs; b) snakes; c) donkeys; d) sheep; e) hens; f) bees

6. *How do they live together?*

a) Wolves live in .... b) Cows and elephants live in ....
c) Birds and sheep live in .... d) Fish live in ....

7. *Quiz: What do you know about ... ?*

Insects

a) Which insect is kept for honey? b) Which insect has no wings, but can hop? It bites. c) Which insect lives in a colony, builds hills and is famous for hard work? d) Which insect can jump as much as six feet?

Mammals

a) Which animal has horns? b) Which animals used to live on the prairie and were hunted by Indians? c) Which animal is called the king of beasts? d) Which animal has given its name to a British luxury car?

Birds

a) Which bird can talk? b) Which bird lays eggs in other birds' nests? c) Which bird is the symbol of the United States?

8. *Here are some colloquial idioms which contain animals. Do you know their counterparts in your language?*

a) take the bull by the horns; b) let the cat out of the bag; c) let sleeping dogs lie; d) as slippery as an eel; e) crocodile tears; f) lead a dog's life

Here are some more difficult ones:

a) a lucky dog; b) as dead as mutton; c) a cock-and-bull story; d) smell a rat; e) blind as a bat

plants around us

166 flowers, bushes, trees · 167 vegetables, cereals, fruit · 168 man and plant · 169 the plant

1. *Letter grid: Put a ring round the ten words for fruits and vegetables. Look for them in all directions.*

Q	I	H	T	K	O	O	B	M	Y	U	T
T	O	M	A	T	O	Q	N	V	O	K	R
B	C	M	V	P	F	Z	Q	T	I	S	I
E	M	J	X	Q	P	Y	M	J	Y	P	A
A	U	D	V	E	R	L	Y	M	L	O	E
N	L	Q	S	N	O	M	E	L	J	T	H
S	P	G	P	I	O	N	N	G	J	A	P
N	U	Q	X	R	P	E	A	O	I	T	Z
X	G	X	A	N	R	R	O	S	I	O	L
P	P	N	T	Z	A	Q	Q	W	X	N	T
G	G	O	F	E	Z	C	C	R	H	V	O
E	H	W	P	M	N	W	I	L	X	R	H

2. *Complete the following words for flowers and trees.*

r __ s __ ;   __ __ k;   t __ l __ p;   b __ rch;   bl __ __ b __ ll;   b __ __ ch;

s __ nfl __ w __ r;   __ sh;   d __ __ sy;   __ lm

3. *Fill in the missing words for the parts of a plant.*

a) Flowers have a stalk. Trees have a .... b) Oaks have leaves. Firs have ... . c) Roses have flowers. Apple trees have .... d) Apples have a skin. Coconuts have a .... e) Nuts have a kernel. Cherries have a ....

4. *Which words often go together? Use each item only once.*

a	dark	1	a(n) ... bark
b	exotic	2	in ... blossom
c	full	3	a(n) ... forest
d	high	4	a(n) ... garden
e	rich	5	... grass
f	soft	6	a(n) ... harvest
g	straight	7	... leaves
h	thin	8	... ground
i	well-kept	9	... moss
j	withered	10	a(n) ... plant
k	mossy	11	a(n) ... trunk

5. *Which word fits the description?*

a) a field where fruit-trees grow: ... (orchard / garden); b) an area of grass in a garden or park: ... (meadow / lawn); c) a piece of land planted with wines: ... (vinegar / vineyard); d) a row of bushes or small trees: ... (hedge / fence); e) the outer part of a banana: ... (peel / skin); f) the branches of a tree grow from it: ... (stem / trunk); g) the part of a plant which is in the ground: ... (root / leaf)

6. *Working in the garden: What can you ... ?*

a) mow; b) grow; c) dig; d) plant; e) pick; f) press; g) fell; h) gather; i) trim

7. *Word building: Find seven new words by combining the 14 words listed below. The new words are spelled with a hyphen.*

apple – buds – orchard – blossoms – trunk – harvest – oak – flower – leaf – rose – tree – cherry – bed – wheat

8. *Here are some English colloquial idioms. Match them with their German counterparts.*

a) to lead someone up the garden path; b) to beat about the bush; c) to be unable to see the wood for the trees; d) to make hay while the sun shines; e) to plough through something; f) to get to the root of the matter

1 den Wald vor lauter Bäumen nicht sehen
2 der Sache auf den Grund gehen
3 jemanden an der Nase herumführen
4 das Eisen schmieden, solange es heiß ist
5 um den heißen Brei herumreden
6 etwas durchackern

earth (a)

170 land · 171 water

1. *Name the continents shown in the pictures.*

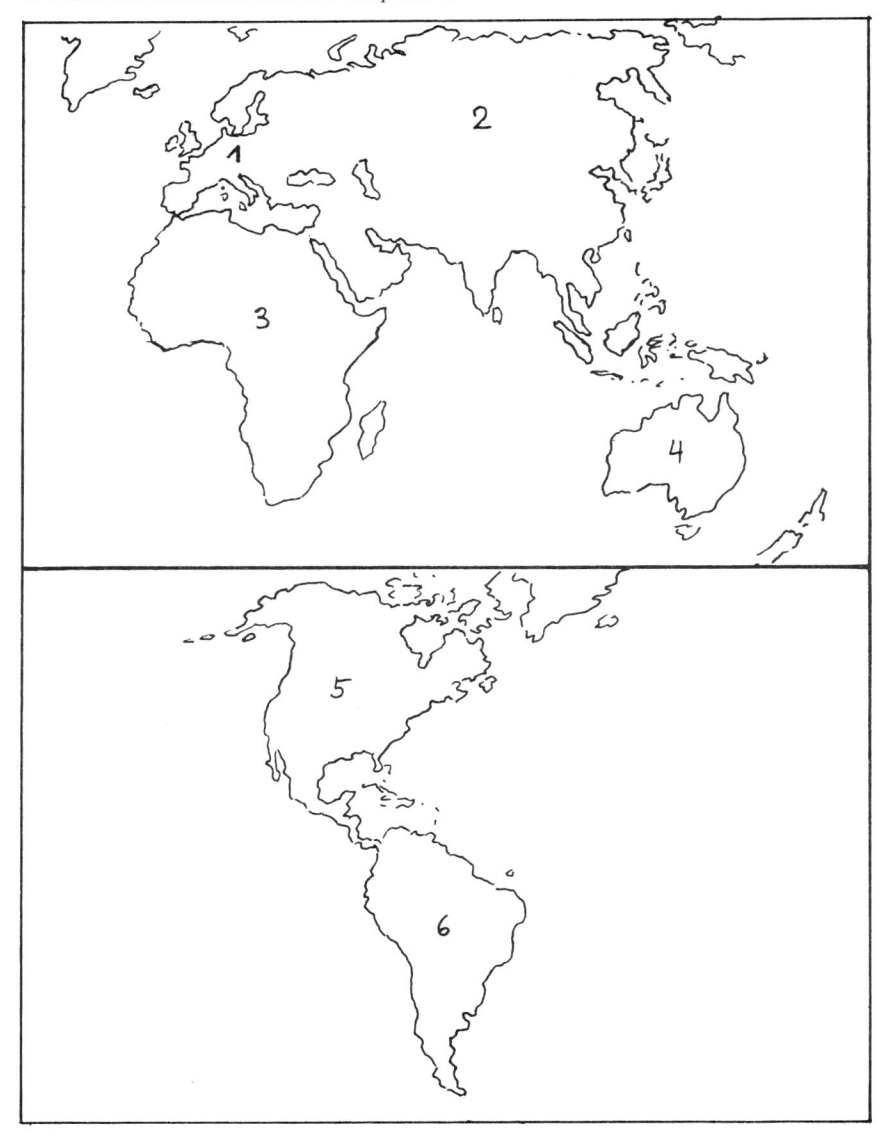

2. *Letter row: Underline the ten hidden words about land and water. They are written like this: → or like this: ←*

e a l l h e l l l i h d g r t m e n t i o n m o u n t a i n d
y e l l o w y e l l a v r e d s s e e d n a l s i j k i r o p a
e b i r c h k c h b e a c h o l d r i v e r w e r q t a z y n c
v a d g a h j u r i e v a w y v e a n h b a n k f d g g a m y n
p l a n e n i a l p l e t a w u c s d f e r t z u i a e a a e s

3. *Word building: Find the 12 geographical names by combining the 24 words listed below.*

Atlantic – English – Great – Gulf – Hudson – Irish – North – Red – River – Rocky – Sahara – Suez

America – Bay – Canal – Channel – Desert – Lakes – Mountains – Ocean – Sea – Sea – Stream – Thames

4. *Find the "odd man out". Try to explain why it is different from the others.*

a river – stream – channel – canal
b shore – coast – cliff – beach
c North Sea – Great Flood – Lake Michigan – Gulf of California
d country – ground – earth – soil
e top – peak – summit – ridge
f sandy – rocky – swampy – stony

5. *Match the adjectives on the left with the phrases on the right.*

a high   1 pass through a ... valley
b stony   2 a ... sea
c rich   3 the ... ocean
d solid   4 an area of ... ground
e shallow   5 sail at ... tide
f strong   6 a ... slope
g rough   7 cross a river where it is ...
h wide   8 swim against the ... current
i pebbly   9 a ... mountain
j steep   10 built on ... rock
k narrow   11 ... ground
l steep   12 a ... beach

6. *Complete the description by adding the missing words.*

The Thames

The Thames is England's best known ... . It ... in the Cotswolds in Gloucestershire. Its traditional ... is Thames Head in the parish of Coates, SW of Cirencester. It ... east towards London. Its length from Thames Head to where it ... into the North Sea is about 210 miles.

7. *Which word fits the context?*

a) After ten days they saw the ... (shore / coast) of Africa. b) Most farms have a ... (pond / lake) from which cattle can drink. c) Brighton is on the ... (sea / ocean). d) He jumped over the ... (river / stream).

earth (b)

172 sky, weather, climate

1. *Word puzzle: Find the missing words and fill the squares with them.*

```
a _ _ _ W
b _ _ _ E
c _ _ _ A _ _
d _ _ _ T _ _ _
e _ _ _ H _ _
f _ _ _ E
g _ _ _ R _ _
```

Here is some help:
a The heavy ... has blocked the roads.
b I'll take an ... in case it rains.
c We could hear the rain ... on the roof.
d A flash of ... makes the sound of thunder.
e It grew ... when the sun had set.
f The most important thing to remember about the weather in Britain is that it is much more ... than on the Continent.
g It's ... with rain.

2. *What's the weather like? Complete the following adjectives and find the nouns they are derived from.*

_____dy   _____ny   _____zy   _____gy

_____ty   _____dy   _____ezy   _____my

_____wy   _____cy

3. *Match the pairs of adjectives on the left with the nouns on the right. Use each item only once.*

a mild / rough   1 ... sky
b thick / grey   2 ... road
c rainy / hazy   3 ... frost
d strong / light   4 ... breeze
e settled / changeable   5 ... climate
f hard / sharp   6 ... day
g hot / burning   7 ... clouds
h light / slight   8 ... wind
i muddy / icy   9 ... sun
j blue / cloudless   10 ... weather

4. *Choose the word that best fits the context.*

a) A barometer shows us if the ... (climate / weather) will change and whether it will be wet or dry. b) Trying to ... (forecast / foretell) the weather is not easy. c) The old tree was blown down in a ... (breeze / gale). d) If the ... (fog / haze) is very thick, we say it's a "pea souper". e) A thermometer is used to measure temperature, usually in the ... (shade / shadow). f) Working in the rain for hours, he got ... (wet / soaked to the skin).

5. *Fill in the right prepositions:* by, from, in (4x), into, of, with, with

a) grey clouds _____ the sky; b) be caught _____ the rain; c) It's pouring _____ rain; d) drive slowly _____ poor visibility; e) tremble _____ cold; f) have ten degrees _____ frost; g) come out _____ the sunshine; h) suffer _____ the heat; i) be struck _____ lightning; j) be deep _____ snow

universe

173 space · 174 space flight

1. *Letter row: Underline the ten words about the universe. They are written like this:* →
or like this: ←

s o n s u n n e m e t o r e a t t e l l e s c t e n a l p m o n
s t r a t s o b s e r v a t o i k o m e c o m e t e w o r l t a
p l a n e f l e e s r o e t e m s c i e n c e g a l a x y a w q
n o o n n o o m m i d n e a h t a d e r t u c o m o r b i t a y
n w n o i t a l l e t s n o c s s o e z o d i a c g h i o p f l

2. *Name the things shown in the pictures.*

3. *Try to explain how they are different.*

a) planet and fixed star; b) zodiac and orbit; c) astronomy and astrology; d) spacecraft and probe; e) space lab and space shuttle; f) the waxing moon and the waning moon; g) constellation and galaxy

4. *Which words often go together? Use each item only once.*

a	put on	1	... the countdown
b	launch	2	... a spacesuit
c	ignite	3	... a course correction
d	overcome	4	... a docking maneuvre
e	land	5	... the first stage
f	begin	6	... the gravitational pull
g	enter	7	... on the moon
h	travel	8	... a spacecraft
i	stop	9	... into an orbit
j	carry out	10	... through space

5. *Word building: Find seven compounds by combining the 14 words listed below.*

age – full – Milky – moon – planetary – rocket – shooting – shuttle – space – space – star – system – three-stage – Way

matter

175 matter · 176 weight, mass · 177 state · 178 texture, surface · 179 temperature

1. *Hidden words: Put a ring round the ten hidden words for elements. They are written in all directions.*

Q	T	Q	F	K	H	L	S	R	X	Q	L
H	Y	D	R	O	G	E	N	N	C	W	B
Q	X	M	I	N	C	P	I	A	Y	O	O
C	R	O	P	N	I	O	Y	R	Q	X	M
H	H	E	I	O	S	T	O	X	Y	X	J
S	C	Z	P	M	S	V	R	G	G	V	U
U	F	W	U	P	Y	T	E	O	G	N	T
L	N	L	N	V	O	N	G	V	G	I	D
P	G	E	N	T	M	C	S	R	N	E	R
H	M	A	O	R	Y	Q	T	Q	I	P	N
U	Z	D	R	L	I	N	O	B	R	A	C
R	Z	Z	I	H	W	T	K	P	X	J	E

2. *Find the "odd man out" in each group. Try to explain why it is different.*

a zinc – iron – sulphur – gold
b oxygen – hydrogen – carbon – radiation
c ounce – gram – stone – hundredweight
d smooth – rough – even – blunt
e crumble – melt – break – crack
f water – air – milk – oil
g flow – boil – bubble – steam
h firm – heavy – hard – strong

3. *What can you ... ?*

grind; crumble; break; melt; spill; light; polish; sharpen; harden; bend

4. *Match the adjectives on the left with the nouns on the right. Use each item only once.*

a	blazing	1	... china
b	heavy	2	a ... needle
c	solid	3	... water
d	delicate	4	a ... surface
e	crumbling	5	a ... weight
f	pointed	6	... air
g	sharp	7	... toast
h	fresh	8	a ... fire
i	bubbling	9	a ... wall
j	rough	10	a ... building
k	smooth	11	a ... axe
l	burnt	12	... silk

5. *Choose the word that fits the context.*

a) Atoms have the power to ... (join / connect) with other atoms. b) The Indian mask was of ... (solid / firm) gold. c) When we opened the picnic basket we found that the ice-cream was ... (molten / melted). d) Water ... (boils / cooks) at 100° C. e) The building was ... (in / on) fire. f) ... (Steam / Smoke) condensed on the inside of the kitchen window.

6. *For each pair of adjectives find a noun that can be used with it.*

a) a hard / a soft ... ; b) a sharp / a blunt ... ; c) a glowing / a warming ... ; d) raging / roaring ...s; e) on hard / solid ... ; f) a good / a worthless ...

7. *Temperatures: Centigrade and Fahrenheit. Convert the following degrees Centigrade into Fahrenheit (To convert Centigrade into Fahrenheit: multiply by 9, divide by 5, and add 32).*

−17.8   −10   0   10   21   25   32   100

Try to find a similarly easy way for the conversion of Fahrenheit into Centigrade.

8. *Put in the right prepositions:* in, in, in, into, into, of, on, on, on, to, to, to

a) made _____ iron; b) stand _____ the scales; c) a pressure of 4 lbs _____ the square inch; d) cracks _____ the ice; e) rain falls _____ drops; f) pour water _____ a bottle; g) be _____ fire; h) be _____ flames; i) burst _____ flames; j) burn _____ ashes; k) something is smooth _____ the touch; l) a scratch _____ the table

existence (a)
180 exist · 181 cause · 182 effect

1. *Complete the sentences, using suitable words.*

a) Does life e... on Mars? b) How did the accident h... ? c) He went to Australia to seek his f.... d) By good l... the door was open and I could go in. e) Things are not always what they s.... f) What was the c... of the fight? g) Did he tell you the r... why he went to London? h) If he doesn't go with you of his own free will, bring him here by f.... i) The s... of the River Rhine is in Switzerland. j) All were suffering from the e... of the heat.

2. *Which words often go together? Use each item only once.*

    a find   1 ... trouble
    b miss   2 ... a reason
    c cause   3 ... the consequences
    d excite   4 ... changes
    e have   5 ... an opportunity
    f influence   6 ... interest
    g take   7 ... a fight
    h bring about   8 ... a chance
    i provoke   9 ... a person's conditions
    j accept   10 ... a person's decision

3. *Word building: Which words can be derived from the following?*

effect; essence; exist; fact; luck; occasion; possible; provoke; react; real

4. *Put in the right prepositions:* against, by, for, for, in, in, of, on, to, to, to, under, under

a) leave nothing _____ chance; b) believe _____ the existence of; c) _____ reality; d) know something _____ a fact; e) _____ condition that; f) _____ no circumstances; g) meet a person _____ accident; h) leave a person _____ his fate; i) be out _____ luck; j) something is necessary _____ life; k) have no cause _____ complaint; l) give the reasons _____ something; m) be _____ the influence of

existence (b)
183 begin, end · 184 remain, change

1. *What are the words? Add the missing letters to find them.*

b __ g __ n; st __ rt; __ nd; st __ p; f __ n __ sh; v __ n __ sh; f __ d __ ; p __ ss; __ d __ pt __ bl __ ; ch __ ng __ __ bl __ ; __ v __ nt __ __ l; f __ n __ l; gr __ d __ __ l; __ ntr __ d __ ct __ ry; l __ st

2. *Which words often go together? Use each item only once.*

a	begin	1	... your work
b	start	2	... a privilege
c	found	3	... a watch
d	stop	4	... a journey
e	finish	5	... a car
f	abolish	6	... law and order
g	continue	7	... a speech
h	maintain	8	... a letter
i	change	9	... the production
j	adjust	10	... a hospital
k	increase	11	... a plan
l	improve	12	... a machine

3. *Complete the sentences, using the words provided. Change their form where necessary.*

adapt, continue, disappear, fall, finish, grow, last, pass, rise, stay

a) The weather ... cold. b) The rain ... all day. c) Prices have ... by 5 pence. d) He was so tired that he ... asleep in front of the TV. e) His condition has ... worse. f) These beautiful birds are fast ... . g) When will you have ... ? h) The week has ... very quickly. i) How long does the film ... ? j) He has ... an old car engine to drive his boat.

4. *Choose the word that best fits the context.*

a) Cut flowers soon ... (fade / vanish). b) Many people say that God ... (made / created) the world. c) How does the story ... (stop / end)? d) Romulus is supposed to have ... (founded / established) the city of Rome. e) I take my ... (final / last) examination next week and then I leave university.

existence (c)

186 action

1. *Mixed letters: Change the order of the letters to find the words.*

aedly; imot; aeehistt; akst; ddee; eopprsu; ceelompt; aekm; cimmott; acchilmops

2. Do *or* make? *Put in the word that fits the context.*

a) _____ a fire; b) _____ your homework; c) _____ the washing; d) _____ a mistake; e) _____ science at school; f) _____ a noise; g) _____ your best; h) _____ a hole; i) _____ a person a favour; j) _____ nothing

3. *Which words often go together? Use each item only once.*

a	delay	1 ... a crime
b	make	2 ... a hotel
c	perform	3 ... a book
d	commit	4 ... an attempt
e	carry out	5 ... a goal
f	manage	6 ... repairs
g	accomplish	7 ... a plan
h	complete	8 ... a journey
i	achieve	9 ... a task
j	do	10 ... an action

4. *What may cause or lead you to ... ?*

a) put off your holidays; b) hesitate to answer; c) avoid hard drinks; d) try a bicycle before buying it; e) accomplish a task; f) sit about doing nothing

5. *Word building: Find words that can be derived from the following.*

act; perform; achieve; accomplish

the order in our world

number

187 calculating · 188 quantity · 189 part, whole

1. *Have one of your group read some numbers aloud. The others write them down in figures, e.g.:*

a one thousand, eight hundred and seventeen
b twelve thousand, six hundred and ninety-five
c sixty thousand and two
d thirty-eight thousand, three hundred and fifty-two
e seventy-seven thousand, two hundred and three
f a hundred and four thousand, three hundred and seventy
g five hundred and one
h two thousand, four hundred and eighty-nine

2. *Now continue in the same way with the following fractions.*

a) two fourths; b) one ninth; c) two and a half; d) a quarter; e) eighteen and fifteen over thirty-five; f) six three fourths; g) twelve eight ninths; h) eight point two three; i) three point three seven five; j) one hundred and twenty-six point five

3. *Read some figures aloud, e.g.:*

24,256   312   40,003   119   88,756   12,980   1,256,785   8,002

4. *Go on in the same way with the following fractions.*

1/2   1/3   2/7   16/35   12 1/3   .56   0.8   34.2   26.08   .12   14.6   0.209

5. *Here is a list of the planets showing their mean distance from the Sun (in miles). How far is Mercury / Venus ... from the Sun?*

Mercury	36,000,000
Venus	67,000,000
Earth	92,900,000
Mars	141,600,000
Jupiter	483,400,000
Saturn	886,300,000
Uranus	1,782,400,000
Neptune	2,792,900,000
Pluto	3,671,900,000

6. *Make a list like the one shown below with the names of the continents in the order of their size and continue the sentences.*

The size of the continents

The largest continent is Asia. It has an area of 17,170,000 square miles. The smallest continent is Australia. North America is twice as large as Europe, which is the second smallest continent. Did you know that the Antarctica is not very much smaller than South America but still larger than Europe? And, as we all should know, Africa is larger than America.

17,170,000 square miles	Asia
11,684,000	...
9,816,000	...
6,878,000	...
5,171,000	...
4,056,000	...
2,944,866	...

Asia comes first; it has an area of ... square miles. Next in size is ... with ... square miles. Then ...

7. *Here are some telephone numbers in words. Write them in numbers.*

a double six two five one
b eight three eight double two
c double four nine oh one
d two nine three oh eight

8. *Say these telephone numbers. If the numbers are in groups, say them in groups, otherwise say each number separately (01 means it is a London telephone number).*

01-822-5050; 1655; 01-246-6488; 2738; 0865-56567; 147-008; 031-332-2904; 141-763; 065-52-7522

9. *Write down your own telephone number and the numbers of the rest of the group, and learn to say them in English.*

10. *Practise with a partner.*

– What's your telephone number?
– It's ...
– Thank you. Mine's ...

11. *Match the pairs of adjectives with the nouns. Add an article where necessary. Use each item only once.*

a odd / even   1 ... people
b large / small   2 ... piece
c big / tiny   3 ... sum
d little / a lot of   4 ... number
e some / several   5 ... time
f considerable / small 6 ... quantity

12. *Quiz: What is the name of the town? Read the following text aloud.*

It is a town in Warwickshire, famous as the birthplace of William Shakespeare (1564–1616), 91 miles N.W. of London by road. It stands mainly on the left bank of the river Avon at the point where it is crossed by a 14-arch stone bridge, which dates back to the reign of Henry VII (1485–1509). There is also a 19th-century bridge. The town was mentioned as early as 691. The group of buildings by the river known as the Shakespeare Memorial comprise a theatre (opened in 1932) that was built to replace the one destroyed by fire in 1926. The library with its 10,000 volumes is one of the most complete of its kind. April 23, the date of Shakespeare's death, is annually celebrated with a procession.

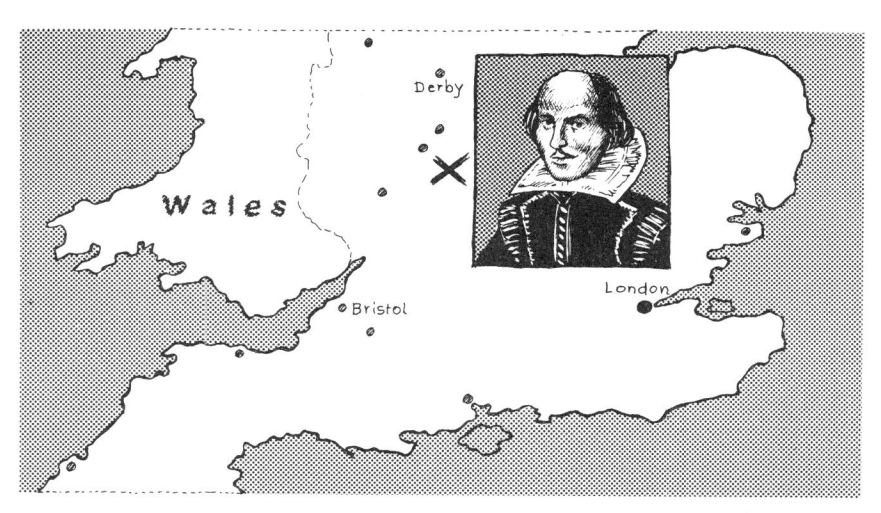

13. *Put in the right prepositions:* at, between, by, in, into, into, into, of, of, to, to, with, within

a) be good _____ figures; b) count _____ twenty; c) divide eight _____ two; d) a number _____ ten and twenty; e) amount _____ £20; f) plenty _____ money; g) be short _____ food; h) divide _____ three portions; i) _____ a fraction of a second; j) break sth _____ pieces; k) buy _____ bulk; l) share a room _____ a friend; m) cut an apple _____ two halves

time (a)

190 clock · 191 day · 192 week · 193 year

1. *Hidden words: Put a ring round the names of the twelve months. They are written in all directions.*

T	L	I	R	P	A	J	H	L	H	C
S	E	P	T	E	M	B	E	R	I	N	N
W	A	Q	G	F	H	V	R	V	S	Q	D
O	Y	X	S	C	E	M	U	Y	E	E	I
N	M	R	R	T	N	B	S	K	C	J	M
O	G	A	A	U	M	P	R	E	Z	U	X
V	M	Q	T	U	Q	E	M	U	R	L	W
E	P	H	S	L	N	B	N	X	A	Y	Y
M	I	O	U	Y	E	A	Q	U	Q	R	R
B	A	O	G	R	F	H	J	T	J	N	Y
E	I	Y	U	X	R	E	B	O	T	C	O
R	C	T	A	K	Z	C	V	F	T	Q	P

2. *What are the words? Put in the missing letters to find them.*

c __ o __ k; __ atc __ ; __ __ ur; m __ __ __ t __ ; n __ __ __ ; __ ig __ __ ;

w __ __ k; __ on __ __ ; s __ __ i __ g; __ um __ __ r

3. *What time is it? Practise this dialogue:*

– Excuse me. What time is it?
– It's a quarter to ten.
– Thank you.
– You're welcome.

Now do the same for the following times:
9.05   12.15   2.35   4.20   8.15   1.10   2.40   11.20   8.45   6.50   12.00   11.50

4. *What time do these trains leave? Say each one in words and in figures (5.30 a.m. = half past five in the morning = five thirty a.m.).*

8.00   8.15   8.27   8.30   8.45   22.50   23.06   24.00

5. *Write down your own timetable for the day. Start with getting up and finish with going to bed.*

6. *What is your school timetable like? In Germany school usually starts at 8.00 a.m. and finishes at 1.00 p.m.*

7. *Put in the right prepositions.*

a) _____ five o'clock; b) _____ the evening; c) _____ weekdays; d) _____ night; e) _____ two weeks; f) _____ noon; g) _____ the daytime; h) _____ Monday; i) _____ the morning; j) _____ the afternoon; k) _____ sunrise; l) _____ January; m) _____ summer; n) _____ midnight

time (b)

194 when? · 195 how often? · 196 how long? · 187 calculating: ordinal numbers

1. *Dates: Say these dates aloud.*

5th January 1940   13 Dec. 1940   March 5, 1966   14/2/1968   17th October 1980

2. *Complete the sentences, using the words:*

ago, before, by, ever, meanwhile, on time, over, recently, until, yet

a) I'm on holiday _____ the twenty-first. b) I don't need to leave _____ –; I can stay a little longer. c) Please be here _____ three o'clock. d) I've seen the film _____, but I want to see it again. e) How long _____ was that? f) Have you seen Tim _____? – Yes, I saw him yesterday. g) We'll go out when the rain is _____. h) The bus came _____ _____. i) You cook lunch – _____ I'll light the fire. j) Have you _____ been there?

3. *Choose the word that fits the context.*

a) I haven't seen him ... (for / since) years. b) Man did not use metal in the Stone ... (Age / Time). c) The President of the U.S. is elected for a ... (period / term) of four years. d) We ... (spent / passed) our summer holidays in Walton on the Naze. e) Queen Victoria was the queen who had the longest ... (term of office / reign) in British history. f) Except for a few sunny spells, it rained ... (continuously / continually). g) Scientists say that we'll have colonies in space in the ... (near / next) future. h) Tim has been away for the ... (past / passed) few days. i) Hurricanes are ... (often / frequent) here in summer.

4. Still, yet, *or* already? *Put in the correct word.*

a) Oh, you're _____ here? I thought you had already gone. b) Oh, you're _____ here? I thought you would come an hour later. c) Have you met Professor Hawkins _____? d) Nothing is known _____. e) I left very early in the morning, and the children were _____ asleep. f) The children were so tired after the birthday party that they were _____ asleep at eight in the evening. g) I've seen the film _____. h) Have you finished? – No, not _____.

space (a)
197 position, direction · 198 line, distance

1. *The compass: Name the four main points of the compass.*

2. *Here are some cities and towns that are very popular with visitors to Britain. Look at a map and supply the missing words in the sentences below.*

a) Bath is to the ... of London. b) Cambridge is 56 ... N.E. of London by road. c) Canterbury is not very ... from London and only 16 miles N.W. of ... . d) Edinburgh, the capital city of Scotland, stands on the ... side of the Firth of Forth.

Try to gather some information about Chester, Exeter, Norwich, Oxford and York and write similiar sentences.

3. *Draw the following.*

a) a straight line; b) two parallel lines; c) a zig-zag line; d) a right angle; e) a wavy line; f) a spiral line; g) a crooked line

4. *Letter row: Put a line under the hidden words used to say where something is. They are written like this:* → *or like this:* ←

d e r t a b o v e a b u w t e r a u n h j u n t e r r e d n u r
d o w n u p s t a i r s h i l l b e d b e s i d e w h e r e i s
a y b g i m k l o p w q x y s d b e t w n e e w t e b m i n u t
o u t e r o u t s i d e i n s i j h s f d n u o r r o w t o w a
a c h e c r e a c r o s s s t u o n h e a d e r o f e b u p s t

5. *Let's play charades: Put the pieces together again to find seven words we use to show position or movement in the vertical sense.*

a – be – bove – der – down – head – hill – low – over – stairs – un – up – up – wards

6. *Complete the sentences with suitable words.*

a) Tim is 5 ft 8 ins t.... b) The building is 40 ft h.... c) How f... did you go? d) A snail's shell has a s... form. e) The river w... through a narrow valley. f) You cannot see Tim's house from here; there is a b... in the road. g) I don't know where I am. Which d... is north? h) The d... from London to New York is 3,200 miles. i) A s... line is the shortest distance between two points. j) One mile is 1760 y..., or 1625 m....

7. *Which words often go together? Use each item only once.*

a	behind	1	swim ... a river
b	through	2	turn ...
c	across	3	sit ... a table
d	downstream	4	hide ... a tree
e	to the right	5	jump ... a fence
f	by	6	walk ... the canal
g	around	7	go ... the streets
h	over	8	side ... side
i	along	9	go ...
j	inside	10	sail ...

space (b)

199 plane, square measure · 200 solid figure, cubic measure, capacity · 201 size

1. *Draw pictures to show how they are different.*

a) angle and triangle; b) square and rectangle; c) circle and oval; d) cone and cube; e) pyramid and cylinder

2. *Mixed letters: Change the order of the letters to find the words.*

alov; ccleir; eubc; rrenoc; dthwi; edtph; aoglln; malls; hint; ceertn

3. *Name the parts of the circle.*

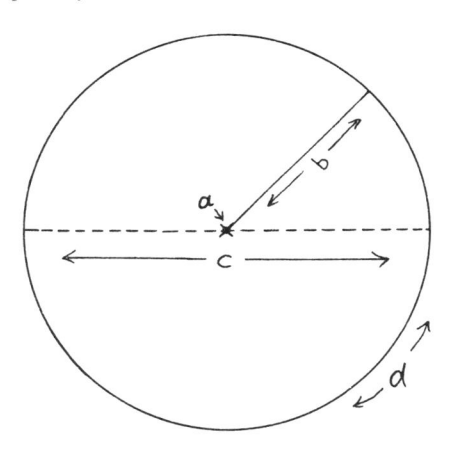

4. *Which words often go together? Use each item only once.*

a	flat	1	a(n) ... area
b	both	2	a(n) ... river
c	large	3	a(n) ... wall
d	broad	4	a(n) ... plane
e	deep	5	on ... sides
f	empty	6	a(n) ... road
g	horizontal	7	a(n) ... hall
h	thick	8	a(n) ... bottle
i	spacious	9	have a(n) ... surface
j	enormous	10	a(n) ... plain
k	vast	11	a(n) ... slice
l	thin	12	a(n) ... amount

5. *Find at least two nouns which can be used with each of the adjectives.*

a) a small ... ; b) a thick ... ; c) a big ... ; d) a thin ... ; e) a minute ... ; f) a huge ...; g) a vast ... ; h) a gigantic ... ; i) a large ...

6. *Fill in the missing prepositions:* at, in, in, in, of, on, on, on, to, within

a) _____ the right side; b) stand _____ a circle; c) six inches _____ diametre; d) a cupful _____ tea; e) sink _____ the bottom; f) _____ a radius of three miles; g) stand a thing up _____ edge; h) _____ full length; i) _____ the depths of the ocean; j) _____ both sides

Lernwörterbuch in Sachgruppen

Emploi des mots
Neubearbeitung

von Diethard Lübke
Best.-Nr. 33300   200 Seiten

Mit ca. 4000 Stichwörtern umfaßt dieses Lernwörterbuch ein geringfügig adaptiertes *français fondamental,* das um ca. 550 Wörter erweitert wurde. Ab Klasse 9 einsetzbar.

Emploi des mots Übungsbuch

von Diethard Lübke
Best.-Nr. 33259   162 Seiten

Das Übungsbuch bietet parallel zu jeder Sachgruppe Aufgaben zur Übung, Festigung und Anwendung des Wortschatzes.

Lensing
Verlag Lambert Lensing GmbH
Postfach 10 50 51 · 4600 Dortmund 1

Lernwörterbuch in Sachgruppen

How to Use Your Words
Neubearbeitung

von Carin Pollmann-Laverentz und Friedrich Pollmann
Best.-Nr. 23300   344 Seiten

Dieses Lernwörterbuch umfaßt etwa 5800 Hauptstichwörter sowie alle wichtigen Ableitungen davon.

How to Use Your Words Übungsbuch

von Friedrich Pollmann und Timothy Sodmann
Best.-Nr. 23254   88 Seiten

Das Übungsbuch zum Lernwörterbuch kann etwa ab Klasse 9 zur Übung, Festigung und Anwendung eingesetzt werden.

Lensing
Verlag Lambert Lensing GmbH
Postfach 10 50 51 · 4600 Dortmund 1